Competitive Business,
Caring Business

Other books by DARYL S. PAULSON

Walking the Point: Male Initiation and the Vietnam Experience

Applied Statistical Designs for the Researcher

Handbook of Topical Antimicrobials: Industrial Applications in Consumer Products and Pharmaceuticals (Editor)

Topical Antimicrobial Testing and Evaluation

Competitive Business, Caring Business

*An Integral Business Perspective
for the 21st Century*

DARYL S. PAULSON

PARAIEW PRESS

NEW YORK

Book and cover design by smythtype

ISBN: 1-931044-39-2

Library of Congress Catalog Card Number: 2002109518

for ROD A. MARSHALL
Mentor, Friend, and Advisor

Contents

Foreword

Daryl Paulson's *Competitive Business, Caring Business* is one of the first of what will surely be many approaches to a more comprehensive or integrated approach to business. As a pioneer in this new and exciting field, Daryl's presentation has much to offer. It is fresh, provocative, and daring. Although I do not necessarily agree with all the details—who does?—it is based on sound theory and research that anyone can test in the laboratory of his or her own business world.

Daryl's approach also makes liberal use of my work, specifically, the integral model that I have developed based on extensive cross-cultural research into human capacities. On the basis of this extensive research, I and my colleagues arrived at a "comprehensive map of human capacities." This comprehensive map—which Daryl will introduce in the following pages—offers a way to make sure that any endeavor, from business to education to medicine, is "touching all the bases" when it comes to various problems and their solutions. Any complex problem demands a comprehensive approach—and if you have a truly comprehensive map, then you are much more likely to succeed in any area.

Daryl is applying this comprehensive or integral approach to business, and therefore he is offering one of the very first integrated business models. As you will see, this is not simply yet another business approach, but rather one that includes and integrates all of the major business models to date—from systems theory to emotional intelligence to corporate culture. The result, far from being unwieldy, actually distills the essence of each of these models into a comprehensive, integrated, elegant approach that has the best chance, by far, of succeeding in the real world—simply because it takes into account all of the others and then moves forward even more efficiently and skillfully.

One of the exciting things about an integral approach to any field, including business, is that there is much room for innovation and pioneering exploration. Truly integral approaches are just now starting to come into existence, and that makes this an exhilarating field. Daryl's work is not only helping to pioneer these approaches, it is stimulating others to create their own versions, which is what any good book should do, and for which I believe we all owe Daryl a deep bow of appreciation.

Ken Wilber
Boulder, Colorado

CHAPTER 1

Going Through the Motions

Sitting in this airport lounge overflowing with business people, I am surrounded by many upbeat, aspiring, successful people. Or am I? Why do they need to drink? It's only 11:05 a.m. I look deeper into the faces of these individuals and I begin to see a different picture. Under the blush makeup of the attractive, middle-aged woman to my left, I am struck by her disenchanted eyes. And, to her right, the sharply dressed man in a blue suit has a look, just beyond his smile, of despair—of meaninglessness. I haven't seen that since my combat days in Vietnam. And the couple just in front of me, obviously married but not to each other, seem to have escaped from this life to a better, more joyous one, if only for today.

"What has happened?" I ask myself. Why is it like this? The economy is good, jobs are plentiful, and Wharton and Harvard business schools have life's answers, which we learn in their pricey, streamlined professional development seminars.

But I know what's wrong, deep in my heart; it's the same thing that's wrong with so many of my peers. There is lack of meaning, lack of substance in their lives. They know they are merely dispensable tools. Their value is only in what they are perceived as producing, not who they are. They keep their mouths shut and deny the injustices they see, they feel, and they know. And I remind myself that "at least in Vietnam, you knew when you were shot. In business, you can be half-dead before you even know you're a target. I remember being exactly in this place several years ago."

I wrote this while sitting in a lounge at Chicago O'Hare International Airport waiting for a flight in the summer of 2001. Business people, like so many others, before September 11, 2001, were consumed with managing their portfolios, accumulating more wealth, brandishing power, controlling their life environment, looking good, and living in denial—denial that their lives lacked meaning, as did their professions.

Then came September 11, 2001. Both the North and South Twin Towers of the World Trade Center in New York City were destroyed by terrorists, as, too, was a section of the Pentagon in Washington, D.C. It seemed as if the United States was unraveling. Scenes of panic, smoke, death, and dust were everywhere.

But, out of the depths of fear and despair, Americans rose. New Yorkers, not known for their compassion, were volunteering to help rescue workers any way they could—carrying the dead and wounded out of the rubble, bringing ham sandwiches and bottled drinking water to firefighters, and helping those who were showing photographs of missing friends and family in hopes of finding them. Throughout New York, citizens responded with bravery, generosity, and a deep authentic sense of community. That sense of community—care and concern—reverberated throughout the country and has continued to do so.

Many business people, not generally known for philosophical thinking, felt helpless like many Americans in the face of this tragedy and began to question what they were doing—their work and their lives as a whole. Is life really just a game of survival? Must dog eat dog? Can there be no meaning beyond making money and acquiring power, both of which can be lost in a heartbeat? Is there a way that matters by which I can contribute, not just to my family, but to my neighbors, the truly disadvantaged, my peers, my country—to the global village?

A growing number of business people have begun answering

these questions in an altruistic manner. No longer is their goal solely to look out for *number one*—themselves—but now, it's also to contribute to the greater good in a particularly novel way—through their business practices. Interestingly enough, altruism is not the serving of others at one's own expense. It is, instead, cooperating for mutual gain (Post, 2002). Biological altruism makes the survival of the group more probable than does just looking after one's own interests. For example, prairie dogs, upon seeing danger, emit a shrill warning sound. This gives their own position away, but enhances the survival of the group. Psychological altruism enables individuals to benefit others, as well as themselves. This is the win-win position we will discuss repeatedly in this book.

Business people have begun openly discussing their feelings of emptiness and lack of meaning with friends, family, peers, and, perhaps most importantly, with themselves in contemplation. Business people, being business people, people of action, have not stopped with the "talk." Now, they are "walking the walk." Their former ways of greed, self-aggrandizement, and acquiring money are not enough to satisfy them. Personal meaning and value are necessary now, with the clear realization that, since human life is temporary, there is no time to waste in vacillation.

One way to accomplish this task—contributing to human betterment through business—is the topic of this book. While intentions are good, solid theory, "do-able" technique, and consistent practice in honing one's business skills are required to make such a contribution. We will discuss this in depth, shortly, but before doing that, let us look deeper into our situation, which psychologists call our "thrown life condition."

Because we humans from the beginning have been "thrown" into an often-hostile environment that challenges our very existence, we have had to find and develop ways just to physically survive. Over the eons of our evolution—and I speak not just of physiobiological evolution, but also social, cultural, and individual evolution—we have devised ways of successfully transforming the raw material—the stone, mud, and water surrounding us—into the tools we need for survival. And we have flourished in this endeavor. Now, mere physical survival is no longer enough, but our ways of surviving, so useful in the past, now interfere with the quality of our lives.

We must ask ourselves how significant is the acquisition of even more money in the grand scheme of things, when we humans are ever more unhappy, unfulfilled, and without meaning? How valuable are more technological advancements when more and more individuals face unemployment or are sentenced to menial jobs? Money cannot, by itself, increase the *quality* of our lives; that must come from inner meaning. We—all of us—have inadvertently, even unknowingly, established the acquisition of money as our highest goal and ignored inner meaning, hoping to substitute it with material progress.

We are helped along in our delusion by science and technology, continually pushing material "progress." While contemplating a life that is logical and mechanical, we have tried to eliminate our concern for emotions, values, beliefs, and ethics. For example, when Chicago physicist Richard Seed announced he would attempt to clone a human being, he emphatically defended his decision by saying that it was required for "scientific progress." Concern for its ethical implications or its impact on cultural and/or personal beliefs, values, and religious tenets was not even addressed.

Psychologists Roger Walsh and Frances Vaughan remind us of important human dimensions we have forgotten and need to revitalize: "while evidence of our intellectual and technological genius is all around us, we have seriously underestimated ourselves. In part because of the blinding brilliance of our technological triumphs, we have distracted and dissociated ourselves from our inner world, sought outside for answers that can only be found within, denied the subjective and the sacred, overlooked latent capacities of the mind, imperiled our planet, and lived in a collective trance—a contracted, distorted state of mind, that goes unrecognized because we share it and take it to be 'normality'" (Walsh & Vaughan, 1993, p. 3).

We have suffered, on a large scale, from lack of positive meaning. God is dead, as Nietzsche stated, and having lost religious faith and the humanistic values bound up with it, we have focused on material values (Fromm, 1968). Yet, at a gut level, we intuit there is more, and we want to find it. Unfortunately, in the past, that quest was rarely finished as more pressing concerns like finding a life partner, finding a higher-paying job, and rising up through the corporate ranks preoccupied us. Far too many of us never seriously question where we are in life, let alone take responsibility for our situation in it. Often, not until we are old do we look back at our lives, perhaps filled with broken images and broken dreams, to evaluate them. But then, it's too late.

The events of September 11, 2001, may have served as a wake-up call. True, people want to contribute to humanity, but we must be aware of what the pioneer of altruistic behavior, Pitrim Sorokin, warned of in the 1950s. "Group altruism," a phenomenon very common today, occurs when the people in a group demonstrate care and concern for those in that group, but indifference to those outside the group.

Sorokin characterized in-group altruism as tribal altruism: "An exclusive tribal solidarity—known as tribal patriotism, tribal loyalty, and tribal altruism—has mercilessly set man against man, and group against group. It has killed more human beings and destroyed more cities and villages than all the epidemics, hurricanes, storms, floods, earthquakes, and volcanic eruptions taken together. It has brought upon mankind more suffering than any other catastrophe" (Sorokin, 1954, p. 461).

If you look around you'll see the effects of tribal altruism today; political systems struggle against political systems, religions against religions, races against races, rich against poor, in-group against out-group. In this book, contribution to humanity crosses all borders focused on humans in their variety of situations.

Formerly, individuals entering the work force learned quickly that money is like a game score. The more you have, the more competent you are credited with being. Is it any wonder, then, that so many have aspired to higher salaries, larger bonuses, and big stock options? At least in principle, these material rewards are intended to make one feel good. Sadly, that is not how it is. Individuals, try as they will, have great difficulty actually translating material wealth into value, meaning, aspiration, contentment, self-esteem, and love. There is a good reason for this. Subjective attributes cannot be measured in physical, objective terms (Wilber, 1995). Furthermore, in our society, grounded in science, which views the physical environment and its objects as the true and only reality of our lives, hopes, feelings, and concerns are not as they appear to those owning them; in reality, they are but mere biochemical reactions.

Psychologists tell a different tale, arguing that feelings, meaning, love, and values—subjective aspects—are absolutely critical to human life. In point of fact, they say that the majority of people they counsel have become dysfunctional, depressed, anxious, unhappy, and unfulfilled because they lack love, understanding, and genuine care and concern . . . all subjective values (Angyal, 1965; Teyber, 2000).

Viktor Frankl, a Jewish psychiatrist interned in several Nazi concentration camps during World War II, wrote about these effects first-hand (Frankl, 1959). Initially, as a strict Freudian, he had no room for the importance of subjective value in life. But he soon discovered that, when prisoners lost their life's meaning—a purely subjective value—they died. This is an important finding that rejects the position that subjective aspects have "no reality."

We humans function in at least three life dimensions that are important, in and of themselves. One dimension cannot be substituted for another. These dimensions include one's personal subjective experience (subjective), the physical environment or existent world (objective), and one's subjective relationships with others (intersubjective) (Alexander, 1982; Davidson, 2001; McCarthy, 1978; Wilber, 1995; 1996; 1998). Science and academia tend to view only the objective dimension as real; psychologists and postmodern philosophers—particularly existentialists—view one's subjective experience as the most real; and social scientists tend to view shared cultural views—cultural relativity—as the most real. However, a growing number of original thinkers and critical theorists—Jürgen Habermas, Charles Taylor, Donald Davidson, Jeffrey Alexander, and especially, Ken Wilber—have repeatedly argued against these reductionistic views, favoring a multi-perspective approach, valuing all three life domains equally. Additionally, they argue that each of these domains is valid, in and of itself, and that one domain's reality cannot be reduced to and explained in terms of another.

This book subscribes to this multi-dimensional view and will employ it throughout. But, for now, let us examine how it is that one domain—the objective—came to be viewed as the sole reality.

The early Greeks, Plato included, identified and differentiated human life into three interdependent spheres, "the Beautiful, the Good, and the True" (Copleston, 1993). For Plato, as well as Aristotle and Plotinus, the beautiful represented art, aesthetics, and personal valuation, as well as the expressive currents within one's being. The good represented morals, justness, and ethics and resided in the intersubjective shared space of human relationships. Science, the study of objective reality, represented, in a very general sense, objective truth—that is, truth according to dispassionate standards derived from observations, not merely the truth according to one's valuation, cultural valuation, or religion.

Over time the interdependence of these spheres or domains was forgotten or ignored, and eventually the domains came to be considered independent of one another. This, in turn, led to their disassociation and, to a large degree, this has become a chief defining characteristic of modernity. Once disassociation occurred, the sphere of science grew dramatically in both size and influence and proclaimed the other two spheres as not only inferior, but that it—science—was the only true sphere. When science extended its boundaries to include philosophy, it became known as "scientism." Scientism contends that the only way to obtain truth is through objective measurement and so the other two spheres (which rely on hermeneutics and phenomenology) were dismissed as inferior modes of knowing.

Scientism is, for the most part, the present major worldview, or paradigm (Kuhn, 1970). For example, theoretical physicist Michio Kaku, in his book, *Visions* (1997), describes in detail three important scientific revolutions: quantum physics, biotechnology, and computer development. Kaku states that these revolutions have profoundly reshaped the twentieth century and will continue to transform most aspects of life in the twenty-first century. He goes to great effort to discuss the tremendous changes we will "experience." But nowhere does Kaku discuss this *experience as experience.* That is, he does not discuss what phenomenological attributes—human values, meaning, or feelings–this experience will bring into our life. It is as if human value and meaning, both personal and cultural, do not exist. By eliminating the subjective and intersubjective spheres, Kaku inadvertently reduces all experience into objective events, which by themselves are no more significant than a meteorite crashing into some unknown, lifeless body of dark matter somewhere in the universe. It's just an event without meaning.

In another example of scientism, Russian astronomer Nikolai Kardashev and Princeton physicist Freeman Dyson, when speculating about extraterrestrial civilizations, categorized them in terms of their level of technological development (Dyson, 1979). A Level I civilization is one that can utilize the energy of its planet to attain its energy needs. This includes geothermal power, solar power, wind power, water power, and fuel power. Such a civilization can mine the oceans and extract energy from the center of its planet. A Level II civilization can mobilize the energy of its planet, and utilize stellar energy as well. For this level of civilization, solar and within-galaxy travel to nearby star systems is possible. A Level III civilization can employ the energy of its planet, star, and galaxy, a requirement necessary because it needs more energy to run than a single planet and star can provide. At this level of technology, true intergalactic space travel is certainly attainable. Interestingly enough, this classification system focuses solely on the technological ability of civilizations. No mention is made of increased levels of wisdom, increased psychological development, greater moral development, a more-just political system, or increased spiritual levels of growth. Whether this is an oversight or a purposeful gesture, again, the subjective and intersubjective spheres are ignored.

Erich Fromm, a prominent psychoanalyst, predicted this problem in the 1960s, as he saw it emerging from our technologically based society (Fromm, 1968). According to Fromm, even then, we had lost control of the social systems we created and ever more relied on machines (i.e., computer-modeling) to make social decisions for us. And in doing this, we have reduced our social goals simply to produce and consume more. This has also led to our losing the capacity for deep emotional experiences and the joy and sadness that accompany them.

According to psychotherapist Rollo May (1953), we humans

search for meaning where it cannot be found—in the material world. Searching for meaning through materialism has created networks of loss of meaning, loss of meaning in one's self, one's interpersonal relationships, and one's relationship with the natural world. Ultimate meaning in life for many was reduced to the sole pleasures of:

Eating well,

Playing well,

Making love well (Gerard, 1995).

Charles Handy (1998), economist and professor at the London Business School, states that while our world is composed of super-efficient and highly productive organizations, it is "soulless and dull." Handy argues that life must include an inner dimension—specifically a psychospiritual one—blended with authentic and loving relationships with others. And he is not alone in this concern.

Thomas Moore (1992), a popular post-Jungian psychotherapist and author who once trained for the priesthood, reports that human complaints are at an all-time high, particularly feelings of emptiness, meaninglessness, and depression that spring from disillusionment about life, loss of inner spiritual values, lack of personal fulfillment, and spiritual hunger. According to Moore, these symptoms also reflect a general loss of "soul"—depth, value, and meaning—in our lives.

Clearly, then, we, as humans, live not just in objective space, but also within our own subjective, inner domain; we share both with our fellow humans.

CHAPTER 2

Applying Multiple Dimensions in Our Lives: The Quadrant Perspective

K en Wilber, a brilliant human science theorist, has written extensively concerning the importance of the three domains of life—the Good, the Beautiful, and the True—which he calls the "Big Three," and has provided an easy-to-understand and comprehensive model that integrates them (Wilber, 1995; 1997; 1998; 2000a; 2000b; 2002). Wilber describes the subjective in "I" terms, the intersubjective in "We" terms, and the objective in "It" terms.

Let's apply this to scientists, who measure and evaluate data objectively acquired through controlled experiments (for example, what Michio Kaku discussed earlier). They focus on the "It," or objective sphere. Yet, those "value-free" scientists value and derive personal, subjective meaning ("I" sphere) from their "objective" work. They also use commonly accepted scales of measurement shared among scientists in that field ("We" sphere) and communicate in symbols of shared meaning with their peers. Indeed, the very language they use to communicate is rooted in the "We" sphere of intersubjective, shared meaning (Jackendorff, 2002). Yet, for the most part, the scientists performing the experiments ("It" sphere) are oblivious to their involvement in the other two spheres and, hence, inadvertently ignore and, thus, reduce the other two spheres ("I" and "We") to the "It" sphere. Let us look at these three spheres (domains) in more detail, so we can use them to shape a new business model.

It (Objective) Domain

This is the domain of empirical science and technology, which bases its findings on dispassionate standards of observation to discover objective truth. But it is not exclusively the domain of science and technology. Any process of documenting and interpreting objective observations to derive conclusions as to what is "truth" can be categorized in this domain. For example, Western academia attempts to understand the social sciences, business administration, economics, and even one's personal life in terms of objective reality (Borg & Gall, 1989).

We (Intersubjective) Domain

The "We" is the "cultural" domain. The term "culture," as used in this book, is not just a mix of people who happen to share the same social background. Instead, it refers to the interpersonal subjective, shared beliefs, language(s), symbols, goals, and meanings of the group—its worldview (McCarthy, 1978). It is the domain of justice, goodness, reciprocity, and mutual understanding. As Ferdinand de Saussure (1959) has pointed out, culture is so fundamental to humans that, without it, we could not communicate with one another. For example, as I write this chapter, I make marks on a sheet of paper. These marks, or written "utterances," are termed "signifiers." As you read this text, the signifiers (written words) signify (represent) a specific meaning to you. When I write about a "cold" day, you recall from your memory what cold represents (signifies) to you, based upon your unique life experience. However, there are common (cultural) meanings of each signifier that we share; these are termed "referents." Your personal meaning of a "cold day" is bounded within what is culturally construed as a "cold day." Referents are what enable us to communicate accurately and precisely with one another. Culturally constructed meaning is so well known to us that it is usually unconscious and unacknowledged and, to a large degree, taken as absolute "reality" (Searle, 1995). This greatly facilitates communication, particularly in differentiating what is normal and what is not, as well as what is good and what is bad. Social reality, particularly shared values and beliefs, constantly changes. While some of us want instant and sweeping change, culture resists it, thereby providing stability. Without stability, there would be no societies, and without societies, there would be no businesses, for they would fly apart at every disagreement.

Culture also provides its members inner meaning derived from being a part of, and accepted and valued, by the group (Geertz, 1973). If cultural meaning disappears, so does personal meaning and, when that happens, a person dies. As described earlier, this is precisely what Viktor Frankl (1959) observed when interned in several different Nazi concentration camps during World War II. When fellow prisoners lost their shared meaning, they lost their will to live. Once that happened, they would usually die within a day or two. Cultural values are not, then, "niceties"; they are "life's blood" for humans.

In the past, culture provided moral structure for its members. Individuals, society-wide, knew what was expected of them to be considered a just and good person. But cultural structures in this country are still oscillating from the cultural revolution of the 1960s. During this period, an entire generation rejected the "then" traditional cultural values, replacing them with free love, drugs, peace, and "doing one's own thing." This trend ultimately forced the culture to split into various subcultures, each demanding its own autonomy and recognition. For more than thirty years, this trend has continued. For example, gays and lesbians have marital rights in a number of states and are no longer expelled from the military. Women and minorities have made stunning progress in acquiring equal rights. Additionally, there have been tremendous advances in ecological awareness leading to pollution control, population control, sound land-management practices, and acceptance of humans as part of the "web of life."

But there is a down side. This diversity has promoted hyperdiversity and helped drive people apart, fragmenting and alienating them. No longer do we aspire to unity within diversity; we now aspire to diversity within diversity (Harvey, 1990). Hyperdiversity spawned a nation peopled by individual, separate, isolated monads who, by erecting psychological barriers, have restricted genuine human interaction—care and concern—among themselves (Wurthnow, 1995). In the aftermath of September 11, 2001, this can change.

But even with the possibility of real change, we fear telling even our closest friends our foibles and vulnerabilities, particularly if we are in a position of social power, for fear of being picked apart in a feeding frenzy of news-hungry reporters, informants, and opportunists. A very common endeavor in our society is to reveal the dirty secrets about our fellow humans in order to deconstruct their moral images and reconstruct them at near "serial killer" level. Robert Merton (1957) studied this phenomenon years ago, in the 1940s and 1950s, and concluded that cultures function, to a large degree, on two levels, just as individuals do. Merton termed these two structural levels "manifest" (surface) and "latent" (deep). Manifest levels of behavior are composed of what members of the culture are consciously aware of and report they are doing. Using the previous example, the immoral actions and behaviors of those in power are exposed in order to remove them from their positions and replace them with moral individuals. But, at a deeper, latent level, unconscious to members of the culture, members all too often are displacing their own guilt and anger about their moral short-comings onto others serving as "scapegoats." By trashing someone else, they provide themselves temporary relief from "self-trashing."

I (Personal) Domain

One's subjective, inner life and its expressions are critical to one's well-being. Yet, throughout our lives—if we are growing developmentally—we find new and more effective ways of relating to the world (Kegan, 1994). Paradoxically, we strive to attain freedom from and, at the same time, unity with others (Angyal, 1965). Through interaction with the objective world, as well as with others, we discover ourselves as physically separate and unique individuals.

Far too many individuals—perhaps the majority of individuals—spend their lives trying to forget about their uniqueness in order to fit into their subculture (Bugental, 1965; Walsh & Shapiro, 1983). This is because they feel inferior, not good enough, and whenever they get in touch with their inner selves, they feel acutely inadequate (Teyber, 2000). To prevent these feelings from coming into consciousness, they avoid encounters with their inner selves by creating distractions, such as working ceaselessly, being constantly occupied with avocational recreation, and even preoccupation with other individuals' problems (Egan, 1998).

Marketing psychologists have consistently used this sense of vulnerability to increase sales by targeting their marketing strategies to sell products that will overcome those individual inadequacies (Paulson, 1997; 1999). Like Merton, they recognize that we, as individuals, function at two levels: surface (manifest) and deep (latent). On the surface, in this case, we have learned to act as if we are competent, sophisticated, intelligent, and "put together." Yet, on a deeper level, the level with which we really identify, we often feel acutely inadequate and try to protect our vulnerabilities. Through marketing, we are offered a way out of these inadequacies. If we use a certain toothpaste, body soap, or cologne, or if we wear certain colors, if we drink a certain beer or wine, or if we drive a certain vehicle, then we will be okay, and we will feel good about ourselves.

Then we will be happy. Yet, when we focus on compensating for our inadequacies or strive to fit into the culture, we often adopt values, beliefs, and goals that just do not fit us as individuals.

So What Are We To Do?

For most of us, before we can act to fix things "out there" to contribute to the world, we need to deal with the inner demons that plague us: our insecurities, our feelings of being bad or not being good enough, lack of direction, lack of meaning, and fear of letting go into life or doing the wrong thing. Dealing with these issues is a long, long process requiring the ability to talk freely with a nonjudgmental friend, mentor, or therapist.

Although there are many ways of dealing with psychological issues—Jungian analysis, Gestalt therapy, cognitive behavior therapy, existential therapy, and humanistic therapy, to name a few—the overriding requirement is that you feel you are *valued and accepted* for who you are. From this stance, self-acceptance is possible. With this self-acceptance, you are in a far better position to contribute positively to social betterment through your chosen field—in this case, business.

The Task Ahead

This business book is both theoretical and applied—theoretical in that it presents the reader with current but time-tested developments in business management and strategy, marketing, systems-thinking, social psychology, psychology, and human science, within the framework of the world marketplace that exists today. It is an applied book in that each of the theories is grounded in research, not mere speculative theory. Many of the newest business theories are not presented, because they have not withstood the test of time. And, while grounded in mainstream business perspectives and practices, this book presents the material in both horizontal and vertical dimensions.

From a horizontal position, we live in a world not composed of separated parts, but of parts comprising a whole, which is, itself, a part of a greater whole. Let me provide an example. A whole atom is part of a molecule; a whole molecule is part of an organelle; a whole organelle is part of a cell. We also will modify the "Big Three"—subjective, objective, and intersubjective—by including a part/whole element. This application will produce a quadrant perspective that is more applicable for explaining business phenomena.

Allow me to first use you as an example of this "quadrant concept," a concept we will apply repeatedly. As you can see in Figure 2-1, your subjective and objective components make up the whole you. Additionally, this whole is part of a collective society and a culture. Note that none of these quadrants can be reduced to or explained by any other quadrant; all are necessary, in and of themselves.

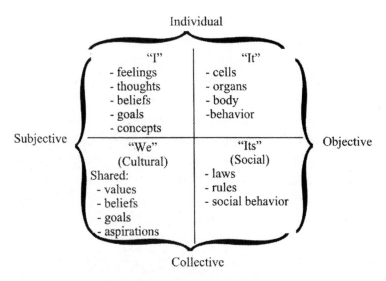

Figure 2-1. Quadrant Model of You

The upper left quadrant represents your subjective, or interior, experience: your thoughts, intentions, and core beliefs, your moral and ethical views, your identity, and your feelings. Although this life dimension is usually ignored in business literature to make it *more real, more scientific, more objective*, it is, nevertheless, a most important one. For example, if your job no longer holds meaning for you, your negative feelings—which are subjective—can impact not only your life, but also your peers' and your work performance. And, although we like to think we make decisions objectively, psychologists argue otherwise (Fadiman & Frager, 2002). Important decisions are made by mixing feelings with objective thought, or by simply acting on feelings and, then, rationalizing them intellectually.

The upper right quadrant represents the personal objective domain, including one's body, one's physiological structure, one's organic brain structures (of limbic system and neocortex, for example), and one's observable behavior. The lower left quadrant represents shared, "intersubjective" attributes such as values, meaning, aspirations, and worldviews held by one's groups, one's cliques, or even one's entire culture. The lower right quadrant represents collective social behavior and the social rules, regulations, and laws that govern it.

These four quadrants will become exceptionally useful as we discuss the integral business model in increasing detail. The important point to remember is that any situation or experience will have portions of all four domains within it. Hence, we will view the world and the business environment situated in it as having at least these four perspectives at every level we discuss.

Business
From a vertical position, the business environment is hierarchical, beginning with the individual employee, extending to the team, to

the company, to the industry, and, finally, to the collection of all industries that make up the environment. Individual tasks are discussed in terms of knowledge and experience required to perform one's job adequately, usually in the objective quadrants. Skills managers need include:

1. Technical skills (e.g., finance, accounting, writing)
2. Managerial skills (e.g., MBO, Theory X, problem-solving, delegating, etc.)
3. Interpersonal skills (e.g., communication, negotiation, ethics, cross-cultural knowledge, etc.)

The team (or group, section, division), the next hierarchical level addressed, is managed and evaluated in objective aspects such as:

1. Performance (output), financial ratios, return on invested capital
2. Costs (budgetary constraints), fixed, mixed, variable, tax structure, capital structure
3. Efficiency (economies of scale, assembly techniques.)

The company as a whole is also evaluated in objective terms, including:

1. Output (sales)
2. Costs (capital and operating)
3. Bottom-line performance (net profit)
4. Dividends paid to stockholders and stock market value.

The industry is generally viewed and evaluated via strategic terms, relative to a company, including:

1. Competitive strategy (e.g., cost leadership, differentiation)
2. Core competencies
3. Global and transnational strategy, foreign direct investments, licensing
4. Strategic alliances and partnerships.

Finally, industries operate within the world environment, generally depicted in terms of:

1. Economics (macro and micro)
2. Industrial substitutes (e.g., chicken instead of beef)
3. Political climate
4. Legal environment
5. Social environment.

Interestingly enough, while there are large amounts of information available in each of these categories, few individuals in a firm, if any, are versed in the knowledge of the entire vertically hierarchical structure, or in all four quadrants at any one of the levels. Instead, the focus is usually on one vertical level and one quadrant, usually the objective. This is a hugely restrictive approach.

Let us now discuss each group depicted by levels 1, 2, 3, and 4 in the vertical hierarchy, using the relationships between the individual and the team, then the individual and company, then the individual and industry, and, finally, the individual and the world (business) environment.

Putting it all together, the structure of this book might look like this (Figure 2-2).

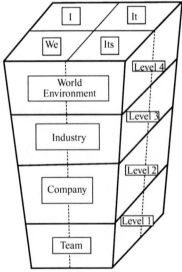

Figure 2-2. The Entire Business System

While it appears that these levels are separate from one another, as we ascend the scale from team to world environment, each higher level—higher in that it is more inclusive—the company transcends but includes the team; the industry includes the company and team yet transcends them both; and the world environment transcends the industry, while also including it.

Note that, within each of these levels is nested the four quadrant regions of I (personal subjective), We (intersubjective collective of that level), It (personal objective), and Its (objective collective of that level). Each of these levels and quadrants interact among one another. Let us now examine the levels one by one.

CHAPTER 3

Individual-Team Level

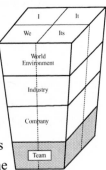

Each business level we discuss in this work consists of a specific relationship between the individual employee and the collective of that level, which may be a team, a company, an industry, or the world environment at large. It is important to realize that, at each level, it is the *individual* who is in relationship with these collectives, not individuals with a team, a team with a company, or a company with an industry. The individual is the core factor of the team, the company, the industry, and the world environment. It is the relationships between the individuals, who take specific actions, dependent upon the situation addressed, that make the collectives (Figure 3-1). For example, if not enough product is produced, individuals at the team level, or even at the company level, evaluate the situation and take action to increase production.

It is important to note there is no one "right" way to respond to

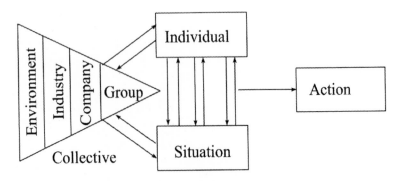

Figure 3-1. Individual-Collective Relationships

a specific situation. Instead, there are multiple ways that provide multiple solutions. However, solutions are always bounded by specific constraints (e.g., economic, capacity, etc.) to create what we will call the optimal solution set. At one time, it was popular to believe there existed one best solution for any specific situation, much like one key fits one lock. In this belief system, all an individual had to do was to link the problem to its corresponding right solution (Figure 3-2).

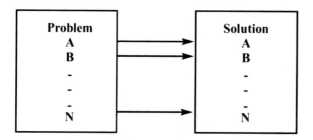

Figure 3-2. One Problem, One Solution

This "lock-and-key" belief system continues to be a fundamental tenet in the eyes of many, particularly in academia and government bureaucracies (Gardner, et al., 2001). However, with some explanation, individuals usually can be trained to recognize that there are multiple solutions to a problem. This can give the person greater leverage in problem-solving, a large practical value. However, even when acknowledging the reality of multiple solutions to problems, a solution set visualized only in terms of objectivity will provide an incomplete picture. Problems and their solutions include subjective and intersubjective components that relate to the individual and the collective group. Hence, when a problem is encountered, the problem has its roots, in varying degrees, in the four human life dimensions (subjective, objective, individual, and collective). Each solution set, then, must include consideration of each dimension (Figure 3-3).

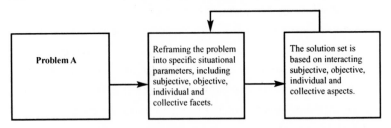

Figure 3-3. Multiple Solutions to a Problem

In this book, we will view solution sets from a four-quadrant perspective (Figure 3-4). There is nothing magical, nor sacred, about viewing business from a quadrant perspective, but the process provides a simple yet comprehensive means for encompassing human reality. We will discuss the quadrants individually for ease of understanding them, but, in reality, they are not separable from one another. With this said, let us begin.

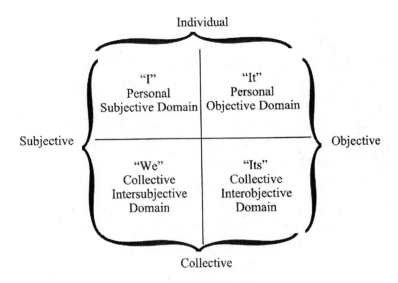

Figure 3-4. Quadrant Perspective

Individual Objective

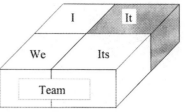

At the team or group level, the individual objective quadrant is the focus of Theory X-style man-agement practices such as Management by Objectives, as developed by Peter Drucker (1964, 1967) and refined by George Odiorne (1969). Management by Objectives (MBO) is an objective, *results-oriented* management style. It provides managers with effective tools for carrying out the three basic aspects of management: 1) planning (goal setting) to meet the objectives, 2) implementing the plan to meet the objectives, and 3) reviewing the results relative to the objectives. For example, if I have a planned goal of producing 700 widgets per day, production of those 700 widgets is the objective. It is expected in MBO that diversions and obstacles will arise, threatening to delay the production goal. I, as a manager, need to have prepared for future problems via contingency plans so I can keep the production objective a reality.

A useful schema of the basic MBO contingency planning approach is presented in Figure 3-5 (Odiorne, 1969). Using this approach, I first need to define the potential problems, as I see them—one at a time—and identify potential causes. I then can formulate options available to me to solve the problem. Notice MBO uses the format of one problem equals one best solution. It is useful to rank these solutions based upon 1) my perception of their contribution to solving the problem and 2) their costs. The option that I think provides the greatest contribution to solving the problem, at the lowest cost, is selected, put into practice, and re-evaluated over time for problem-correcting results. While this model may be simplistic, it is useful in many situations, particularly when one cannot get bogged down in analysis. MBO can be supplemented via management tools, such as quantitative analyses, described in Management Science texts (Hillier & Lieberman, 1980; Lapin, 1991; Render & Stair, 2000).

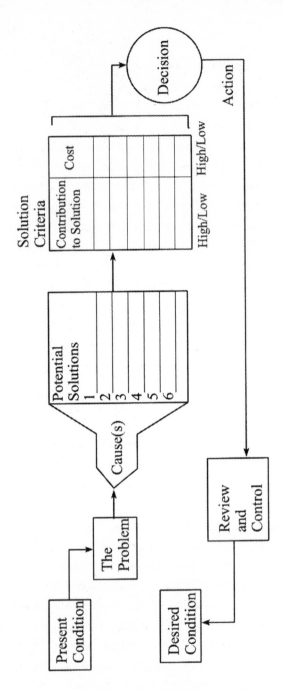

Figure 3-5. MBO Problem-Solving Model

Quantitative methods employ mathematical models, most often statistical ones, to help determine the optimal course of action (e.g., greatest payoff with least risk) and are easy to employ using a computer. Quantitative methods can be used in solving current problems and even predicting business and economic conditions in the future. Linear and multi-linear regression, moving average, weighted average, and exponential data-smoothing time-series models are commonly used for forecasting future sales (Neter & Wasserman, 1974). The use of these models can help attain the desired outcome of both the short-term and the long-range strategic planning for an organization (Bowerman & O'Connell, 1979; Paulson & Van Woert, 1984). Additionally, more complex time-series forecasting methods such as Box-Jenkins procedures can be used to predict business trends with and without cyclical and seasonal trends (Makridakis & Wheelwright, 1978).

Quantitative models are useful for setting product-inventory levels, based upon historical demand patterns, costs of storage, procurement costs, opportunity costs, and spoilage costs. The most common variety is the inventory decision model called the Economic Order Quantity (EOQ), which is really a family of models using the supply and demand economic principles as their basis (Lapin, 1991; Paulson & Vogel, 1984; Paulson & Van Woert, 1984; 1985).

Another useful family of quantitative methods is linear programming (not to be confused with computer programming). Linear programming, a system of analytical methods, is used to determine the optimum "product mix" to produce to maximize profit or minimize costs (Paulson & Van Woert, 1985). For example, in the pharmaceutical industry, linear programming is used to predict what mix of tablet dosage levels (25mg, 50mg, 150mg, and 250mg tablets) to produce in order to maximize profit or minimize cost for a particular drug product.

Quantitative methods such as Program Evaluation and Review Techniques (PERT) and Critical Path Management (CPM) procedures are also valuable to determine the optimal process steps to take in building homes, hotels, airplanes, rockets, and entire space launch programs (Dilworth, 1979; Lapin, 1991). And, finally, Bayesian decision analysis is valuable in complex decision-making processes to select an optimal course of action, given a number of options and expected payoffs of those options (Lapin, 1991).

The Theory X management style presents a view that employees are generally unmotivated. From this view, employees need to be supervised closely and need work-tasks assigned to them in a well-structured manner, contained in a stable work environment. Employees want to take breaks, eat lunch, and leave work at specific, regular times; they want a routine. Because Theory X practitioners view most employees as not being self-motivated, employees will not voluntarily grow on the job. For example, they can become more valuable to the company and attain greater personal growth through self-study or off-site education but will rarely do so (Hersey & Blanchard, 1993). Additionally, Theory X assumes that most employees do not want to shoulder more job responsibility, and that most employees have little capacity or desire to solve job-related problems, let alone do so creatively.

From a strict Theory X perspective, employees, for the most part, are motivated to work mainly to meet their physiological needs (those basic needs required to sustain life—food, clothing, shelter, etc.) and their safety needs (freedom from fear of physical danger and losing their ability to meet their physiological needs) (Barnard, 1968). Finally, those who subscribe to this management style assume employees must be controlled closely and even coerced in order to achieve organizational goals and objectives (Drucker, 1967, 1974).

From a person perspective, the basic unit of the Theory X managerial focus is the individual employee but can be adapted to a group, team, division, or the entire organization. Popular Theory X management practices include task management styles, management by objectives, as we have discussed, various military styles, most structured management styles of blue-collar workers, and management practices within government agencies (Drucker, 1974; Hersey & Blanchard, 1993).

Individual Subjective

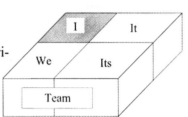

An individual's subjective experience, including his or her various self-developmental lines, such as role-taking abilities, held beliefs, constructed worldviews, cognitive development, moral development, special talents (e.g., music, sports, etc.), life goals, aspirations, psychological defense mechanisms, emotional capacity, creativity, altruism of a "spiritual" kind (such as care, openness, concern, and religious faith), communicative competence, kinesthetic skills, and gender identity, to name a few, are represented by this domain. Some of these developmental lines, perhaps all, evolve hierarchically, that is, via increasingly complex and inclusive stages. At any one time, a person is at various stages of growth for each of these lines of development. Let me illustrate this and, for simplicity, I will use just three levels of developmental growth, called pre-conventional (below the cultural norm), conventional (the cultural norm), and post-conventional (above the cultural norm), and three lines of development—cognitive, moral, and logic-mathematical (Figure 3-6).

Figure 3-6 depicts one possible configuration of a person's levels of development. What it illustrates is that individuals may be highly developed in some aspects of their psychic development, but less so in others. The illustration indicates an individual who is highly developed cognitively, able to apply not only formal opera-

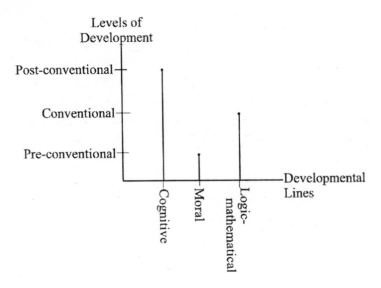

Figure 3-6. Lines and Levels of Development

tional skills, but also higher, post-formal processes, such as visionary systems thinking, where one applies formal operational thinking skills to different systems—politics, finances, and science—and integrates these. This individual, however, is lacking in moral development—looks out for number one, has shady dealings, or takes advantage of others, etc.—and average in logic-mathematical development. As one can imagine, for an individual, the complete configuration of the various lines of development is exceedingly complex. Because individuals vary in level for each line of development, this will impact their understanding, motivation, and behavior in the workplace.

From a business perspective, the individual subjective quadrant is represented best by Theory Y-type management, a participative style that emphasizes the need to attain both business and personal goals. Theory Y management styles focus on motivating employees through "buying into the objective" to attain specific business goals (Osterberg, 1993; Stoner, 1982). Individuals who employ

Theory Y assume that work is as much a human need as eating and sleeping. That is, employees need satisfaction from creative, important, and quality work. Therefore, if an employee does not perform to expectations or needs to be motivated to do so, the work conditions, not the employee, are considered unfavorable to high-quality work performance (Gibson, et al., 1979). Advocates of this management style also argue that individuals not only want to work but are innately self-directed to be productive, particularly if their working environment is conducive to achieving success. Additionally, those favoring Theory Y management styles argue that the vast majority of employees are not only capable of solving problems arising within the scope of their job functions, but they desire to do so.

From a Theory Y perspective, employee motivation to work goes beyond satisfying Maslow's physiological and safety needs to satisfying "higher needs," which include social needs (the need to belong to and be accepted by the work group), esteem needs (to be both valued and recognized as important by their work group, feel self-confident, and feel important), and self-actualization needs (to develop one's innate potential).

This is not to say that Theory Y practitioners see no value in meeting physiological and safety needs; instead, they argue that employees want more out of a job than just a paycheck. They want to belong to a group, be valued by that group, and develop their innate potentials. Finally, Theory Y proponents believe that employees, when properly trained, do not require close supervision and certainly not coercion to achieve organizational goals. They will work via self-direction, given adequate motivation (Maslow, 1954; 1971). Motivation, as used by Maslow, centers around enabling workers to realize that it is beneficial for them to achieve organizational goals because, by doing so, their own goals will be met. It is important, then, for managers to work with employees to discover how their personal needs may be met through performing organizational work. Once this has been accomplished, little more needs to be done, because the employee will be self-motivated and self-directed to perform quality and timely work.

However, it takes time for employees to truly realize that performing organizational tasks can also fulfill their personal needs (Kelley, 1985). But the process can be accelerated by skillful managerial mentoring and helping the employees "match up" personal needs and group goals, which are intertwined.

Personal needs can also be categorized structurally as "surface" and "deep" level needs. Simply stated, surface level needs are conscious to the individual, while deep level ones are not. For example, when questioned why they work hard, employees may state that they want to make more money, a surface level response. However, at a deeper, unconscious level, for example, employees may work hard to meet needs for self-esteem, i.e., they feel better when accomplishing something that matters to them and their group.

However, there is a danger in motivating through need attainment; that is, misidentifying impulses as needs. Studies have shown that many conscious impulses are not readily useable by Theory Y managers (Hershey, et al., 1996). Relative to impulses, one needs food, now; one needs play, now; one must buy something, now. These kinds of need impulses, technically termed "maintenance needs," are not significant, long-term motivators.

Needs also are individual-specific. For example, in order for a person's social needs to be met, genuine feelings of acceptance by the group are not enough. Acceptance must also come from certain individuals within the group in a particular way; not just anyone or any way will do. Self-esteem needs often require years of personal development to be satisfied (Angyal, 1965; Schneider & May, 1995). Self-esteem requires that people not only feel good about themselves and their job performance, but that they "walk their talk"—they get things done. Further, it requires that individuals work with their "shadow" side. The shadow side of a person embodies traits, beliefs, and desires of which one does not want to be aware (Jung, 1969). For example, if people present themselves as competent but know that they really do not have the qualities they profess to have, this is shadow awareness. Generally, individuals cannot work through their shadow issues by themselves, because they are too self-threatening. Also, because people do not let their shadow issues come into their consciousness, due to the defense mechanisms of repression and denial, working through these issues with a competent guide in counseling or psychotherapy is necessary (Monte, 1977; 1999; Teyber, 2000). The practical importance of working through shadow issues cannot be overemphasized. Unacknowledged, shadow issues generally get in the way of individuals by making them appear hypocritical. Why? Because what one does not acknowledge in oneself, one frequently acts out in interactions with others (Bandura, 1997; Bugental, 1965; Egan, 1999; Teyber, 2000). For example, people might complain mercilessly about the lack of common courtesy others extend, but then they are unaware of their own blatantly discourteous acts toward others.

It is important that managers who desire to employ a Theory Y management style realize that the application process is long, slow, and filled with frustrations. Not only must managers link the goals of individual employees with those of the team, but also must repeatedly enable employees to identify their deeper needs and show them how those needs can be met by performing the job. Often in the learning process, employees "drop the ball" and appear not to be self-directing and self-motivating. This is particularly so for employees just entering the workforce. They have been told specifically what to do, when to do it, and to what degree for so long that doing something on their own is often unfamiliar and confusing to them. This is a normal problem of transition, requiring patience and persistence.

Specific needs are not static; they change over time. What people need in terms of meeting their self-esteem and self-actualization requirements at one stage in life will surely change in another. It is wise to be aware of and be attentive to change dynamics, so that as employees grow and develop as individuals, they can also be guided to grow and develop smoothly within the team group.

Finally, a word of caution. All too often, managers fall victim to trivializing employees' needs. For example, self-esteem is sometimes trivialized to mean doing the job "satisfactorily," social needs to mean being "one of the guys or gals," and self-actualization to mean winning a trip to an exotic South Pacific island. Needs, particularly deep needs, are much more individual-specific and complex than this.

Organizational Culture (Team) Management

This quadrant is the management focus of the organizational team, as a whole, in terms of its shared values, goals, meaning, and aspirations. It is based upon the phenomenon that, when human groups interact, a culture emerges—that is, a collective of individuals who share similar values, goals, and beliefs (Argyris, 1964; 1993; Newman, 1997). Using organizational cultural management principles, one attempts to influence a group's beliefs, values, and goals, aligning them with organizational goals. Successful cultural managerial influence requires much time, consistency, and congruence to develop, but once achieved, the culture tends to be very stable.

In 1924, Elton Mayo, a professor at Harvard Business School, discovered first-hand the power of cultural group dynamics.

Efficiency experts at the Western Electric Company in Hawthorne, Illinois, were studying the effects of light illumination on telephone-assembly worker productivity. The efficiency experts assumed that, as illumination was increased, the work output would also increase. To test this, two groups of female telephone-assembler personnel were selected: a test group and a control group. The test group's illumination levels were varied, but the control group worked under a control standard illumination level. As light intensity increased, output levels for the test group increased as expected. Unexpectedly, however, output levels for the control group also increased, baffling Mayo and his team.

They expanded the scope of their research to include a variety of other work conditions, such as providing scheduled breaks, company-furnished lunches, and shorter work weeks, to see what would happen. Productivity kept rising. Then Mayo took all of these benefits away, returning the women to their original work conditions. To his amazement, productivity rose to an all-time high. After much reflection, Mayo and his team discovered that productivity was not merely a response to working conditions, but to human "cultural" aspects as well. Mayo determined that, due to the attention lavished upon the telephone assemblers by the experimenters, they felt important. They no longer viewed themselves as isolated individuals, working physically close to each other, while psychologically distant. They had become participating members of a congenial, cohesive work group, a "cultural group." This elicited feelings of fulfillment, affiliation, and achievement, needs which previously had been unsatisfied. This phenomenon is now known as the "Hawthorne Effect."

Management practices focusing on organizational cultures have been increasingly popular over the past several decades, particularly due to their demonstrated efficacy in Japanese management practices (Deal & Kennedy, 1982; Deming, 1982; Hampden-Turner,

1990; Kanter, 1983). The individuals who make up a team share values, beliefs, goals, and a worldview (Newman, 1997). Through "intersubjective" bonding, they form a culture. As related to management practices, proponents focus on creating an organizational "culture" that shares an organizational philosophy, conducts business within the limits of the organizational philosophy, and performs work within the organizational philosophy constraints (Argyris, 1982; 1992; Ousbourne, 2002). Management practice, as related to organizational cultures, is not focused at the "superficial" level of politeness, rituals, and organizational functioning depicted on organizational charts. Instead, the strength and cohesion of organizational cultural management is derived from truly understanding and then influencing the deep, highly significant levels of the culture—that is, how the organization really operates, whom one can get help from, where resistance will arise, and who will lead (Deal & Kennedy, 1982). To function adequately, management of team cultures requires that both physiological and safety needs are met, and that everyone perceives they are met. The foundation of organizational culture management rests on the human need to be an integral part of a social group, a group that has positive meaning to each member (Maslow, 1954).

It is relatively easy to influence development in a start-up or young company, where there is no established culture. But as time goes on and the culture develops and matures, it takes on a "life of its own," becoming very stable and, therefore, resistant to change—good or bad.

In managing a group culture, its shared values must be addressed, influenced, and shaped. It is necessary, then, that employees not only understand, but actually buy into the organization's philosophy. Otherwise, there will be no underlying meaning to cement the group culture. Managers must also recognize that they are not outside the corporate culture but part of it, too. The actual beliefs, values, and goals (deep structures) of those employees who make up the organization must be congruent with the stated organizational philosophy (a surface structure), and that philosophy must be overtly practiced by management. If not, managerial influence of the culture in terms of desired change will not be possible. For example, it is impossible to expect loyalty from employees when, at the slightest downturn, employees are laid off (Hampden-Turner, 1993).

From another important vantage point, the team's culture provides "emotional" safety for individuals because they do not feel solely responsible or accountable for specific results (Argyris, 1993). They feel, instead, partially responsible, which is both an advantage and disadvantage. It is an advantage in that it can reduce "responsibility" job stress. Many employees cannot tolerate the emotional stress of their job responsibilities by themselves. They need to feel others also share the responsibility to buffer or dilute it, so to speak. With this buffering in place, they function very well. A disadvantage is that a false sense of security exists in that employees tend to feel that someone else is more responsible for the job results than they are. When this view prevails, individual accountability is not present, because individuals do not feel personally responsible to any high degree. It is the task of managers, then, to balance individual ownership with group ownership, something of an art in itself. Managers need to continually remind themselves that the group's culture helps define, through a membership role, personal identity, and provides sustained value and meaning to an employee in terms of values, goals, beliefs—a worldview, in other words (Argyris, 1982). This promotes stability and tends to reinforce a culture's ability to sustain itself over time. And group stability is necessary for it to learn to work as a team (Argyris, 1964).

Finally, organizational cultural management is analogous to

working with an individual employee through Theory Y management practices. But, instead of focusing on an individual, one works with the collective: a team, a section, or a department.

Group Behavior

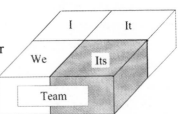

This domain represents the behavior and results of a team as a whole in producing goods and/or services. Group output is generally more than the sum of individual employees' outputs. An emergent factor, or additional characteristic, appears as a result of individuals coming together to work as a self-directed team (Polkinghorne, 1983; Senge, 1990). This is the domain of systems thinking and systems design, and of systems management, which demands a perspective of seeing and accounting for the actions of the whole and the parts simultaneously within the team.

Systems management practices have evolved continually during the twentieth century, spanning fields as diverse as engineering, manufacturing, the space program, medicine, and the social sciences, as well as management theory (Bertalanffy, 1968). A systems management perspective is applied to teams ever more often, as job processes become more complex (Senge, 1990; Sterman, 2000). In systems management, one does not view team tasks as mere sets of linear cause-and-effect relationships; instead, it views them as a system of continuous interdependent influences, relationships, and processes (Bertalanffy, 1968). Systems management promotes seeing and understanding the interdependent relationships among tasks and among individuals' concepts of the tasks, the influences of suppliers, of buyers, of competition, and of rules and regulations, and the dynamic environment external to the task system. While more complex than viewing a task system as separate independent steps, it mirrors the actual world environment more accurately and precisely. Systems management is process-focused rather than static "snapshot"-focused, as found in traditional management.

A key to understanding systems management is to understand that business occurs as a series of interdependent events, not as independent events. That is, Event A influences Event B, which influences Event C and so on. For example, customers ask for a specific brand of wine; this influences the wine buyer to purchase that wine; this influences the store manager to adjust shelf space by eliminating another wine to accommodate the new brand. Just a simple case like this has many interdependent events. In systems management, there are two forces present: forces of change and forces of stability, often called "resistance." In the wine example, the new wine has much appeal to wine customers, so management is motivated to shelve more (force of change). But introducing a new brand requires employees to change inventory labeling, cataloging, and reporting, which they do not want to do (force of stability).

Of particular importance to note regarding the systems approach is that the solution to the current problem will, at some time, create a new problem. For example, I recall an instance where a specific work team—in this case, a department—was ineffective in its order processing. Several management consultants were brought in to "fix the problem," which they did, and then turned control back to existing management. But when the consultants left, the problems worsened. New problems arose from the very solution in which the original problem was rooted. Instead of the department personnel learning to solve and correct their internal problems, they were provided a ready-made solution that did not require they learn to work together to problem-solve. So the apparent solution made the problem even worse.

Working with and within a business system takes time. As energy is put into the system, it takes a certain amount of time to realize the results; there is a "lag" period of, unfortunately, unknown duration

(Gharajedaghi, 1999). The situation is much like being in a warm shower that suddenly turns cold when someone somewhere else in the house turns on a hot water faucet. Immediately and instinctively, one turns the shower setting "up" to provide more hot water, but nothing happens; then one turns up the hot water even more, and still nothing happens. Suddenly, a stream of "scalding" water comes blasting out of the shower head. This is the same conundrum of reactive adjustment faced in business systems. To work with a system effectively requires small, leveraged adjustment iterations and patience, rather than extreme, all-at-once changes. In business, it would be simple if responses to change were immediate, but this is not generally the case. As in the shower analogy, we tend to expect immediate feedback on our business actions to judge their effectiveness. When no response feedback occurs, we then continue making adjustments, often, in the end, resulting in an out-of-control situation. Patience is needed, for the harder one pushes the system, the harder it pushes back.

Is There a Best Style?

Management books and courses argue the pros of a management system in one of the four quadrants just discussed without acknowledging the existence or validity of the others, let alone seeing how portions of each world space are needed optimally to construct the whole management system. Generally, current management styles are versions of Theory X or Theory Y practices, with emphasis placed on Theory X management, as it relates to financial strategies, quantitative business methods, and decision-making (Horngren, 1984; Samuelson & Nordhaus, 1995)

People managers, the organizational "diplomats," often favor cultural styles of management (Hersey & Blanchard, 1993). Those with engineering backgrounds typically favor systems-type management, because it is so similar to the project management styles they apply to engineering jobs of large scale, such as building an airplane or the new Mars spaceship orbiter and landing module (Banathy, 1996). Unfortunately, rooting oneself in one quadrant, often without even realizing the existence of the other quadrants, is seriously short-sighted and will undoubtedly prove to be a competitive obstacle, especially as more individuals come to realize the advantage of an all-quadrant model.

To more completely understand "truth"—that is, "what is"— it is advantageous to recognize that truth is not an absolute, but relative, and that truth is often composed of "multiple truths" (Anderson, 1995). From these multiple truths, one can then synthesize a more inclusive model (the all-quadrant model proposed in this book). By contrast, from the customary way of thinking, termed "formal operations," one realizes only one truth. As a result, the various quadrant styles of management, each rooted in a single quadrant, become antagonistic, in that one management style is assumed to be more true than any of the others. This stance essentially reduces four-quadrant reality to one-quadrant reality. This is much like Viktor Frankl's (1969) argument that, when a multidimensional aspect of the world is reduced to a more simplistic level, the result is several conflicting views. For example, in three-dimensional space, a cylinder is a cylinder, containing both rectangular and spherical components. When presented in two-dimensional space, the cylinder is either a sphere or a rectangle— a self-antagonistic position in which one must be right and the other wrong (Figure 3-7).

A similar limited view of reality causes much debate as to what is the best management style. Should a manager act by getting closer to the action? This is certainly the prescription of Tom Peters (1987). Or how about managing by linking people to one another, as proposed by Warren Bennis (Bennis & Nanus, 1985)? Or what about managing by objective controlling, as championed by Michael Porter (1980)?

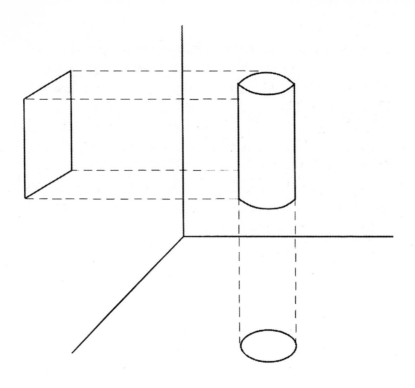

Figure 3-7. Three-Dimensional Object Reduced to Two Dimensions

If one merely manages by getting closer to the action, the focal thrust of the manager all too often dissipates. It goes all over the place. If one leads by linking, the company loses its focus and drive. And, if one leads by objective control, the company may implode. A better way is what Andrew Grove calls "nudging." That is an integration of doing, linking, and controlling which, in essence, is the same position I am taking in integral business, but taking it even further by including both horizontal quadrants and vertical levels. So, at this first vertical level, that of the individual and the team, the relationship can be schematically portrayed via the quadrant model (Figure 3-8).

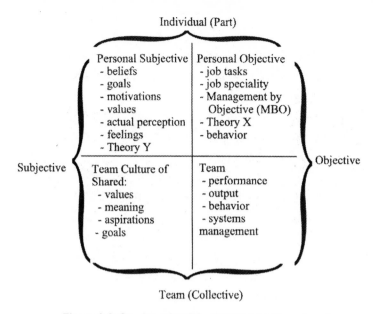

Individual (Part)

Personal Subjective	Personal Objective
- beliefs	- job tasks
- goals	- job speciality
- motivations	- Management by
- values	Objective (MBO)
- actual perception	- Theory X
- feelings	- behavior
- Theory Y	
Team Culture of	Team
Shared:	- performance
- values	- output
- meaning	- behavior
- aspirations	- systems
- goals	management

Subjective .... Objective

Team (Collective)

Figure 3-8. Quadrant Model of Individual-Team Level

A Multidimensional Management Model

As previously stated, the vast majority of managers utilize only one management style and, therefore, address only one quadrant in reality. This limits their effectiveness. However, with the ever-increasing number of competitors and their ever-increasing capabilities challenging present-day organizations, the "one-dimensional" manager is on the way to extinction (Cahoone, 1996; Wilber, 2000b).

Managers, in order to assure their organizations are competitive in the new global marketplace, are wise to adopt a multi-perspective management vision (Anderson, 1995; Kegan, 1994; Sinnott, 1994). This provides a broader, more comprehensive management practice, thereby providing a competitive advantage. There is, however, a cost. *Extra effort* must be made by managers in order to acquire adequate all-quadrant knowledge and be competent in all four management perspectives. Hopefully, over the long term, managers will lead with full quadrant knowledge, employing Theory X, Theory Y, Organizational Culture, and Systems management styles in an integrated manner. With the integration of the four management styles, an "emergent" factor arises, which is more than merely the sum of the four management styles.

Before concluding this chapter, I need to briefly address ongoing development and training that must be established and directed by all management levels.

Developmental Growth Within Each Quadrant

Although each quadrant represents a different management perspective, each quadrant domain—the individual employees, the team culture, and the team system—evolves through focused training, planning, implementation, mentoring, and feedback. Let us look at the multidimensional quadrant model again, this time incorporating multiple developmental stages (Figure 3-9).

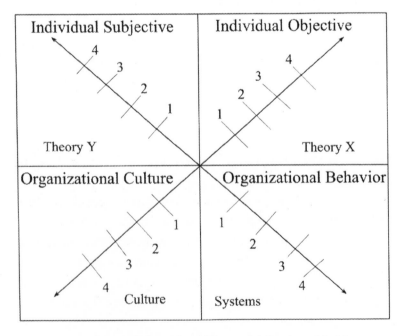

Figure 3-9. Multidimensional Managerial Quadrant Model

Notice that each timeline arrow bears four numbers (1, 2, 3, 4). These represent developmental stages, generally considered to be sequential, invariant, and inclusive (Hersey & Blanchard, 1993). That is, an individual employee or the entire organization must pass sequentially through each developmental stage, not skipping any of them. As the stages are mastered, an individual or the organization will then evolve to the next stage. However, no employee or organization will proceed fully from one stage to another. Instead, they will proceed in degrees through the stages. Perhaps 50 percent of a person's ability, or 50 percent of the organization's, will be in Stage 1, 25 percent in Stage 2, 20 percent in Stage 3, and 5 percent in Stage 4. The stages are not discarded, but integrated with the previous stages as part of the developmental process.

There will be a lag period between individual development and organizational development, as the organization will always be slower to develop than the individual (Argyris, 1964). Finally, note that the four stages in development are equivalent for each management quadrant dimension. The stages are:

Stage 1: The "telling stage." Specific instructions and close supervision are provided.

Stage 2: The "selling stage." At this stage, the instructions are not only given, but also the rationale behind them. Opportunity for clarification is provided.

Stage 3: The "participating stage." In addition to integrating Stages 1 and 2, ideas are shared in this stage, and participation in decision-making is encouraged.

Stage 4: The "delegating stage." Here, the employee or group is proficient in Stages 1, 2, and 3 and job responsibility for both decisions and implementation of a project are turned over.

Now let me briefly go over the stage development process for each of the four managerial styles.

Individual Objective: Theory X (Upper Right Quadrant)

Initially (Stage 1), an employee is trained on what to do, when to do it, and to what degree. Observable performance, as it relates to the job objective, is the key to measuring job success. The employee does not contribute to management at this point, since she or he is learning to perform the job.

Once an employee has become competent in performing a job, she or he can move on to Stage 2. At this stage, the rationale behind the job performance is explained. The employee, over time, will move on to Stage 3, the participation stage.

At Stage 3, the employee has performed the job long enough under various environmental conditions to feel competent. At this point, the employee can actively participate in scheduling, making changes in methods, and trouble-shooting.

Stage 4 is the stage in which the employee can competently perform his or her assigned job, as well as see potential problems that may arise and prevent them. Moreover, she or he can solve unforeseen problems when they arise and can aid others to do so as well. At this level, a person is competent to perform the job tasks on his or her own.

Individual Subjective: Theory Y (Upper Left Quadrant)

Stage 1 encompasses training to do the job, as previously described. The management process also provides the employees with positive coaching that they are competent enough to learn the job. This is a job anxiety-reducing, confidence-building stage.

Stage 2, the selling stage, is when the purpose of the job is explained as well as how doing this job will empower the employee, giving him or her self-confidence. Additionally, the employee will be shown how doing the organizational work properly will be of advantage to him or her personally.

Stage 3, the participation stage, occurs when the employee can help decide how to meet his or her needs on the job, what types of psychological support they need, and whether they want to take on special projects designed to help the organization and meet some of their self-esteem and self-actualization needs.

Stage 4 is achieved when an employee can nurture others who need guidance, as well as contribute to their emotional and psychological support. At this stage, the employee does not need high levels of external praise, for it is internalized. They know, unconditionally, that they are valuable.

Organizational Systems (Lower Right Quadrant)

Here (Stage 1), managers are trained or coached on how to work together in a structured manner, focusing on what the organization must accomplish, when it must be accomplished, and to what degree. Observable team coordination and performance is the center of training in this stage.

Once the management team becomes a competent, cohesive unit, the members move to Stage 2. At this stage, they are trained on how the organizational system works in theory and what they need to do from a systems perspective, as well as training in systems management, both detail and process. Once this has been accomplished, management can participate in restructuring the system, expanding it, combining it with the other systems and, of course, reviewing performance and trouble-shooting problems (Stage 3). When Stage 3 has been mastered, the team is mature (Stage 4) and can learn to govern itself without the direct help of higher levels of management.

Organizational Culture (Lower Left Quadrant)

Stage 1 is the team-building, encouragement phase. It presents an air of positive regard for all employees. It sets precedence that managers and staff can work together without political ploys, etc. This is an anxiety-reducing stage.

Stage 2 is the stage where cultural "whys" are explained. The beliefs, values, and goals are explained to all employees. This stage focuses on social belonging, as well as self-esteem within a unified team.

Stage 3 is the participation stage, in which employees and management can participate jointly in setting cultural values and "organizational views." It is the stage of helping to establish what the values should be.

Stage 4 is that of a mature culture, embodying values, beliefs, goals, and views that are congruent with the organization's goals.

Conclusion

With the increasing number of competitors entering each market, and with each of these competitors increasing their capability levels, it is critical that managers not remain one-dimensional. By learning to expand their management abilities to multidimensional management, and to view change as the only constant in business, they will be in a better position not only to compete and excel, but also to truly contribute to increased quality of life for people throughout the world.

CHAPTER 4

Individual-Company Level

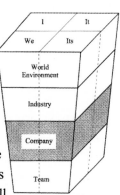

T his chapter addresses the next hierarchical level, that of the individual in relation to the company. Much of what I discussed in the previous chapter (individual-team) is also applicable at this level. The major focus at this level is, of course, the individual's interaction with the company as a whole. Those senior managers who set policy at the company (corporate) level all too often view the individual employees in mere abstract terms, as if they were but shovels or picks. These managers would better serve the employees and stakeholders by recognizing the importance of the individual employee to the firm in a real, non-abstract way. Losing touch with employees can easily mean disaster in the form of employee indifference, passive-aggressive behavior, and disloyalty. Let us now make our way through the quadrants at this level.

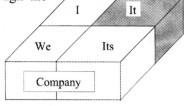

Individual Objective

This quadrant, in simplest terms, represents a single employee's behavior relative to the company as a whole. The individual working at the corporate level must track and, to some degree, manage company output expectations, particularly in meeting budgetary constraints (e.g., costs, hours, head count, overhead, new equipment expenses, etc.). At this level, the CEO and his or her staff focus their efforts on meeting the "numbers," directing the business force, and generating a return on investment for stockholders.

Executive managers are frequently pulled in four directions at one time and complain of not getting anything done (Drucker, 1985; 1993; 1995). They usually must manage their own time and physiological or emotional stresses, for no one else is available to do it for them. Time management is crucial, for there always are more tasks needing attention than time permits. Time management requires that one prioritize essential tasks, as well as learn and practice the art of delegation.

At this level, one must be able to identify quickly key issues that come up and address them as practically as possible. In each decision, a corporate manager ideally takes into account solutions that do not merely maximize profit and/or minimize costs, but optimize them relative to the effect on the company as a whole, its culture, and its impact on the environment.

In order to save time, a corporate-level manager must quickly be able to identify changes in trends on the monthly profit and loss statement and balance sheet. This requires that the manager understand general accounting principles and be particularly adept in aspects of managerial accounting (Horngren, et al., 1999). In managerial accounting, tax credit costs such as depreciation expense and amortization are not that useful, for one is more interested in production costs, cost-benefit alternatives, and target sales. Managerially, variable costs, fixed costs, contribution margins, and selling prices are the general tools (Horngren, 1984). Manipulating them enables one to compute quickly the break-even costs in dollars or items produced, to optimize product/service mixes, to know how much leverage a company has based on fixed costs and contribution margins, and to determine the amount of sales necessary to bring net profit to a specific value.

A manager should have a good understanding of finance to manage a firm's performance (Bringham, et al., 1999; Horngren, et al.,

1999). By far, the most popular yardstick for measuring performance is Return on Equity (ROE), which is simply: $\dfrac{\text{Net Income}}{\text{Shareholders Equity}}$. But generally, in financial analysis, one is more interested in the three component "levers," which combine to make up ROE, often called a DuPont analysis.

$$\text{ROE} = \underbrace{\frac{\text{Net Income}}{\text{Sales}}}_{\substack{\text{Profit Margin} \\ \text{Lever}}} \times \underbrace{\frac{\text{Sales}}{\text{Total Assets}}}_{\substack{\text{Asset Turnover} \\ \text{Lever}}} \times \underbrace{\frac{\text{Total Assets}}{\text{Shareholders' Equity}}}_{\substack{\text{Financial} \\ \text{Lever}}}$$

The profit margin lever, the fraction of each dollar of sales that trickles down the income statement to profit, reflects two things: the company's pricing strategy and the ability to control operating costs (Higgins, 2001). The income statement provides the information to evaluate this lever.

The asset turnover lever, a ratio, measures the sales generated per dollar of assets. The balance sheet provides information to compute this lever.

The financial lever is a measure of "leverage." A company increases its leverage when it raises capital through debt, relative to equity. The challenge is not necessarily to raise this lever value, but to balance debt and equity financing by their total benefit to the firm (Bringham, et al., 1999; Crawford, 2000). In assessing the value of ROE levers, it is probably more useful to perform a trend analysis over several years, looking also at the financial ratios that help to explain the levers (Figure 4-1).

Also, tremendous tax advantages can be had with the proper selection of investment options, depreciation options, amortization, debt/equity financing, and buy-or-lease options (Grinblatt & Titman, 2002).

In concert with accounting and financial practices are business quantitative methods, such as decision models, optimal product mix models (linear programming, simplex programming, integer pro-

$$\text{Return on Equity} = \frac{\text{Net Income}}{\text{Shareholders' Equity}}$$

$\text{Profit Lever} = \dfrac{\text{Net Income}}{\text{Sales}}$	$\text{Asset Turnover Lever} = \dfrac{\text{Sales}}{\text{Assets}}$	$\text{Financial Lever} = \dfrac{\text{Assets}}{\text{Shareholders' Equity}}$
$\text{Gross Margin} = \dfrac{\text{Gross Profit}}{\text{Sales}}$	$\text{Collection Period} = \dfrac{\text{Accounts Receivable}}{\text{Credit Sales per Day}}$	$\text{Payables Periods} = \dfrac{\text{Accounts Payable}}{\text{Credit Purchase per Day}}$
Tax Rate	$\text{Inventory Turnover} = \dfrac{\text{Cost of Goods Sold}}{\text{Ending Inventory}}$	$\text{Debt to Asset} = \dfrac{\text{Total Liability}}{\text{Total Assets}}$
Percentage Income	$\text{Fixed Asset Turnover} = \dfrac{\text{Sales}}{\text{Net Property/ Plant Equipment}}$	$\text{Times Interest Earned} = \dfrac{\text{EBIT*}}{\text{Interest Expense}}$
		$\text{Current Ratio} = \dfrac{\text{Current Assets}}{\text{Current Liabilities}}$
		$\text{Acid Ratio} = \dfrac{\text{Current Assets-Inventory}}{\text{Current Liabilities}}$

*EBIT = Earnings before interest and taxes

Figure 4-1. ROE Ratios

gramming, non-linear programming, inventory models, forecasting models, and queuing methods) (Lapin, 1991; Render & Stairs, 2001). Fortunately, with some understanding of the theoretical basis of these quantitative models, solutions can be generated via most computer business software packages, which vastly assist the manager in application speed, complexity management, and practicality.

Health

This domain also includes physical self-care, which plainly will have first-line importance to the individual (Anderson, 1987). Potentially, there is much emotional stress at the corporate level, contributing to poor nutrition and lack of sleep. Often, time to reconnect with oneself is in short supply. Hence, one must learn to pace oneself for, if one does not, one will simply break down and burn out.

Many executives with whom I work discount self-care and turn the care of themselves over to a physician. That is, they visit their physician at regular intervals. This is not what I have in mind. What I propose is that one not wait to be treated medically, once a clinically diagnosed disease or disorder has been discovered, but take proactive responsibility for one's health. This requires that one become intimately aware of one's body and the messages it sends over the course of the day. For example, when excess muscle tension is felt, a person can attend to himself or herself with a vigorous physical workout, a self-relaxation strategy such as biofeedback, some form of meditation, or time out to do nothing but reconnect with one's body/self (Remen, 1980). None of these actions require that much time, but it will pay off immensely in greater health, as attested by wellness physicians (Anderson, 1987).

Although it is nearly impossible to eat adequately and naturally, for many employees, particularly executives, creative alternatives such as vitamin and mineral supplementation are easily achieved. One can take a multiple vitamin or research various nutritional sources for a tailor-made program.

Regarding physical exercise, both cardiovascular and muscle-strengthening conditioning should be implemented. Many argue they get enough exercise playing golf or walking, but these, in fact, may be inadequate (Cooper, 1989). Many exercise physiologists recommend vigorous cardiovascular exercise at least twenty minutes every other day via jogging, racquetball, handball, treadmill, stair-stepper, or bicycling, stationary or cross-country (Edlin, et al., 1996). Additionally, many claim strength-conditioning is important for the legs, arms, chest, and abdomen by means of a free-weight routine, a resistance machine, or the like (Cooper, 1989).

It is also important to keep emotional and mental perspectives in balance. Many executives I know—particularly men—try to convert feelings into thoughts to better deal with them (Teyber, 2000; Vaughan, 1995). Usually, this strategy is not altogether successful. A healthier way is to acknowledge feelings, particularly those of frustration, and to work through them on an emotional level, as well as by relieving the tension with physical exercise and muscle relaxation techniques such as biofeedback.

Finally, research has shown that those individuals who get seven to eight hours of sleep per night, exercise moderately, keep their weight within normal ranges, do not smoke, and drink alcohol only in moderation not only will live longer but will have a better-functioning body throughout their lives (Anderson, 1987).

Individual Subjective

From an individual perspective, corporate policy and action set the stage for a person's beliefs about the company, how she or he views the company as it actually functions in 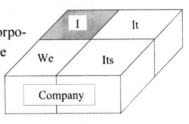 the world. This, then, enables one to determine if there is growth potential, whether his or her values are congruent with the company's, and how far the company policy can be trusted to be fair.

At the corporate level, employees are generally at a number of cognitive developmental levels. Usually, a person can remain employed if she or he is at the concrete level of cognitive development, where a person can perform required tasks adequately, understand the operational rules, and carry the rules out in literal fashion. A person functioning at this level generally will not succeed in supervisory positions, but can carry out other people's requests, as long as they are explained adequately.

But having developed to the level of cognitive formal operations, where an individual can perform at the concrete level, as well as perform formal cognitive operations that entail self-reflective, propositional reasoning, is even better. That is, a person can conceptualize himself in any number of hypothetical situations and conceive solutions to them. Additionally, one can perceive a situation from the perspective of another. Supervisors and managers of teams, divisions, or departments can flourish at this level of development.

However, truly to excel, and not just contribute to one's own wealth at this level, one must develop to the post-formal cognitive level. At this level, one has access to both concrete and formal operational skills as well as the post-formal ability to perceive the organization from a systems perspective—a system of interlinking teams coming together as a unified whole company. Specifically, at the post-formal level, a person not only understands his or her specialization field—finance, accounting, management—but can also link these fields, as well as the product/service knowledge the firm has (e.g., its science and technology), its sales and marketing strategy, and its quality control program (Collins, 1983). At this level, as at the team level, one does not search for "the" solution to a problem, but for multiple solutions. The job is the optimizing of the results, possibly using a combination of solutions.

To link the various teams operationally throughout the company is a huge, on-going task, so it is important that the executive can, through negotiation, attain these results. In all organizations, there is a certain amount of conflict among individuals. For the executive merely to give orders to unit managers can cause alienation, resentment, and resistance among these leaders. To let the team leaders "argue it out" and come to an agreement by themselves may be useful, but often fails to produce win-win solutions. Instead, the more aggressive dominate the less aggressive, at first. But then, over time, the less aggressive tend to "pay back" the more aggressive through passive aggression. Passive aggression results when one perceives a problematic situation and allows it to worsen by doing nothing and warning no one. It is retaliation against the perceived antagonist (Brooks & Odiorne, 1984).

What does work among the groups is to negotiate a solution that is mutually beneficial, and that group members recognize to be so. This is important. If group members do not see its value, it is not beneficial to them. And this stance cannot be a "prop," something with which to "pacify the troops." The agreement must truly have the genuine interests of all members. Negotiations do not need to be done in a fixed, prescribed manner, although that can be very effective. It is often useful to "get out of the box" to meet team leaders' needs in a creative, win-win manner.

Generally, a win-win position makes everyone less reactive and enables one to get something by giving something. Communication experts stress several key elements that must be addressed in successful negotiations. First, the problematic issues must be identified and defined such that each team leader sees these and understands them (Culp & Smith, 1992). Negotiation experts stress that arguing over a "position" is overly restrictive and usually leads to defensive entrenchment, not viable solutions. That is what happened in the early 1960s when then-President Kennedy tried to negotiate a ban with the U.S.S.R. on nuclear testing. A critical question arose in the negotiation process: "How many on-site inspections per year should the U.S.A. and U.S.S.R. be permitted to conduct to investigate suspicious semiological fluctuation?" The Soviet Union agreed to three and the United States wanted more than ten. The talks broke down over these positions, even though the terms of an inspection were never addressed, which was the original objective. Little effort was directed toward the mutually beneficial objective of verifying that no nuclear warheads were detonated. The talks, of course, ended in no agreement. It is important, then, to focus on objectives, not positions, to get a solution.

Second, it is important that issues and people be separated. All too often, negotiations become focused on personalities, not problems (Illich, 1973). Once personalities become the focus, negotiations tend to break down into accusation, justification, and outright "mud-slinging." The result is hurt feelings and resentment on both sides, ignoring the central issue or issues altogether. While in the heat of an emotional negotiation process, it is difficult not to attack personalities. But like most things in life, with practice, refraining from personal attacks becomes easier over time.

Third, it is important that, whatever potential solutions to issues are given, they are assured to be 1) practically achievable, 2) long term, and 3) unlikely to cause further problems in the near future. A condition to re-evaluate the solution in the future is necessary, because, as we have already discussed, the very solutions to today's issues can become issues themselves in the future. Hence, scenario testing, using hypothetical situations that realistically may occur and potential ways of coming together to solve them before they get out of hand, is important.

Fourth, realizing that solutions for today's problems may become future problems can be very valuable to the long-term success of the negotiation process. The negotiating groups need to realize that their current solutions are not absolute solutions. They will need to readdress every issue in the future.

Fifth, it is important that, once a solution is agreed upon, it be formally drafted in a clear and concise manner. If not, new arguments tend to arise as multiple interpretations surface, often creating new rifts.

Finally, whenever possible, it is important that objective criteria be satisfied in the negotiation process, not because they are more real in the negotiation process, but because they provide the strongest and most direct data by which the success of the solution can be seen.

Corporate Objective

This is the level of the entire company's objective output and, of course, it is the major responsibility of the Chief Executive Officer (CEO). Precise goals are formulated and articulated by the CEO and his or her staff, ensured by formal controls to prevent or at least reduce the effects of unexpected negative surprises (Bennis & Nanus, 1985). This requires the integration of the firm's operational components, linking and integrating the teams into a unified whole. In this endeavor, systems management is very useful to assure efficiency and effectiveness of the whole company. This, however, in no way reduces the importance of the traditional linear relationships between the CEO and staff officers in comparing projections to actual numbers, as well as closely supervising the profit and loss statement and the balance sheet.

There are a number of general ways a company, as a whole, can be operationally configured. These include:

1. Entrepreneurial
2. Bureaucratic
3. Professional
4. Diversified
5. Innovative.

Entrepreneurial Organizations. This is a fairly simple structure, not much more than a group of individuals with a central leader and perhaps several managers. Generally, an entrepreneurial organization is young and tightly controlled by the founder and perhaps several associates. Minimal planning and training are required as far as organizational procedures are concerned. There are few, if any, middle managers, for the decisions are handled at the top. Entrepreneurial organizations are generally lean and flexible and exist outside the market domains of the large bureaucratic firms, filling the niches that larger firms ignore. Changes to meet new challenges and fill new niches are relatively smooth and rapid.

Bureaucratic "Machine" Organizations. In this type of organization, jobs are generally highly specialized and standardized. The organization has an elaborate and complex administration requiring a large technostructure to design and maintain its system of procedure standardization. This type of organization has a rigid but stable hierarchical structure, difficult to change. Governments, particularly the federal government, are good examples of this type of organization.

Professional Organizations. This is a type of bureaucratic structure that standardizes skills, instead of jobs, as exemplified by law firms, engineering firms, hospitals, and universities. The management structure is decentralized, with much of the power at the line-manager level (professional staff, such as doctors, lawyers, and professors). Usually, a large staff serves in support of the professionals, and the organization does not closely regulate the professional staff regarding their services. The management structure of such organizations is generally hierarchical, stable, and resistant to change.

Diversified Organizations. This organization structure is a set or collection of independent entities or "divisions," coupled with an administrative structure. These divisions do not produce the same product or service, but they do focus on the same goal: bottom-line profit. With small technostructures, the CEO likely oversees team leaders (e.g., division managers). Diversified organizations have, in the past, been very popular, but with ever more intense global competition, many of these organizations refocus their corporate goals, because they are generally composed of unintegrated, diverse units, frequently having different goals.

Innovative Organizations. This type of organization has aspects of each of the other organizational types, ranging from a highly structured, bureaucratic firm to a loosely structured, entrepreneurial firm. Usually, an innovative firm is structured according to the current needs. That configuration remains operational until an impasse is encountered and the configuration is modified. The innovative firm's operational requirements determine the specific operating configuration. The requirements are, for example, coordination of the work teams (departments and divisions) to assure adequate communication between them.

Let us now look at the various forms of operating structure in a greater detail applicable to all organizations. Henry Mintzberg has developed a very useful way of portraying the essence of organizational structures (Figure 4-2), and each of the organizational configurations just described operate, in some form, within this structure (Mintzberg & Quinn, 1996).

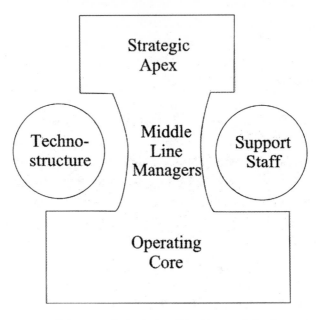

Figure 4-2. Mintzberg's Organizational Model

From this view, each firm has an individual (e.g., C.E.O.) or board that oversees the firm, represented in Mintzberg's organizational model by the "Strategic Apex" position. At this level, the function is not only to link the various teams or groups (i.e., departments, divisions), but to position the firm to compete effectively in the industry not just now, but also in the future. This is a proactive position, where the company is actively engaged in serving its market, positioning itself to be competitive in the industry, and applying new technologies in all areas of the firm's operations to be more effective and efficient. The unique aspects of the firm, its core competencies in providing products or services of value, derive from the firm's technostructure base. And it is often the technostructure that is responsible for the manifestation of core competencies, providing the firm has a competitive advantage. In a small firm, the technostructure may come from the CEO. But, in larger companies, it is expertise in electronic miniaturization expertise, as in Sony's case; for Johnson & Johnson, it is its ability to translate new medical knowledge into a technology; and for a fast food restaurant, such as Burger King and McDonald's, it is the innovation of providing cheap, yet tasty, fast-service food.

Within each firm, a support staff is necessary for its smooth functioning, which includes accounting personnel, secretarial staff, custodians, and maintenance personnel. The firm itself is propelled by an operating core consisting of personnel who carry out the design intentions of the technostructure, including sales personnel who sell the firm's goods and services. There is also a linking component consisting of middle-line managers who coordinate operations between the technostructure, the support staff, the operating core, and the strategic apex.

There long have been arguments about what is the best structural configuration for control and productivity. Before company downsizing became a way of corporate life, most growing companies became increasingly hierarchical, with long organizational chains of command. However, the longer the chain of command, the less efficient a firm is in adapting to emerging challenges in the competitive environment. This has proved deadly to many firms, when they no longer could respond to meet the demands of the environment. Hence, flatter line management has become popular. There is no one organizational structure appropriate for all situations. Instead, structuring should be viewed as a normal, on-going process, dependent upon the business environment.

Corporate Culture

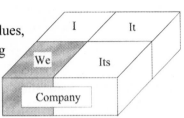

It is the collection of shared values, goals, aspirations, and meaning that make a company's culture. At the corporate level, overall trust in the company is a major factor in determining the makeup of the culture. This can best be summed up as "can employees trust the company (management actions) to act consistently with their interests and concerns in mind—and not just talk about them?" This is generally evaluated by employees observing whether what management says and what it does are congruent, not hypocritical. Trust is the crucial issue, and how it is addressed at the corporate level will trickle down to the team and individual levels, influencing both.

Psychologists specializing in group dynamics tell us that groups are very astute in knowing when they are being taken advantage of (Argyris, 1982; Barnard, 1968; Kolb, et al., 1983). Group members may, on the surface, seem not to acknowledge a threat, but at a deeper level, employees may be planning a retaliation for the perceived "unfair" situation. In a very real sense, corporate culture provides the container that "holds" all of the team cultures. This is a double-edged situation, having both positive and negative effects. For example, if massive layoffs, downsizing, and other kinds of actions perceived to be "anti-employee" occur without apparently real care and concern for the employees, the corporate culture will, more than likely, lose positive cultural strength. Employees may show up for work, say the right things, and perform just enough work to remain employed, but passively aggress company interests whenever the opportunity presents itself (Gibson, et al., 1979).

Because corporate culture evolves over a long time period and is rooted in the firm's actual and perceived actions and policies, molding a "pro-company" corporate culture requires that a CEO be critically aware of the true importance of corporate values, and that these exist on at least two structural levels: surface and deep (Hampton-Turner, 1990). Recall that surface values are what the company says–its "policy." Deep values are what the company does. If a company proclaims its people are its strength, yet lays off 10,000 employees, then its deep and surface values are at odds. And it is at the deeper level where the true corporate culture is rooted. Values that are shared, not just proclaimed, determine the culture. The firm, then, must not only state, through public relations, that it appreciates its employees, it must demonstrate that appreciation in genuine action.

Given a firm has coalesced its stated values into truly shared ones, a firm can influence its culture by establishing a corporate vision. That is, into what does the company want to develop? A vision must inspire all employees, all the way up to the CEO, to contribute to its realization. It must, therefore, be a vision that matters because it means something (Wall, et al., 1992).

The next step is to actualize the vision into the world through business operations. And, finally, the values of the company must be reinforced over and over by walking the corporate talk.

Before leaving the company level, let us discuss a key contributor toward company success—Total Quality Management (TQM).

Total Quality Management (TQM)

Total Quality Management systems, a style many companies are currently adopting, had its roots in Japan in the 1950s. After World War II, W. Edwards Deming went to Japan to help take a population census. The Japanese had heard about his statistical quality control theories and quality management perspectives in general.

A number of Japanese companies invited him to teach them his methods, so he did. Deming described, in great detail, the importance of top management quality leadership, customer/supplier quality partnerships, and continuous quality improvement in new product development and manufacturing processes (Deming, 1982). Japanese management embraced Deming's ideas, and the rest, as they say, is history. Unbelievably, Deming resided in Washington, D.C., his entire adult life, but remained virtually unknown nationally until 1980.

Another key figure in TQM is Joseph Juran, who also taught quality control principles to Japanese firms in the 1950s. Juran focused his program around three key areas: 1) quality planning, 2) quality control, and 3) quality improvement.

And, finally, the third important TQM originator is Philip B. Crosby, a corporate vice-president of quality at International Telephone and Telegraph, and the originator of the Zero Defects concept. Deming, Juran, and Crosby have been likened, respectively, to a fire-and-brimstone preacher, a theologian, and an evangelist. Table 4-1 provides a highlight comparison of their philosophies (Evans & Lindsay, 1999).

Deming and Juran speak of training to improve the quality system by controlling variability to provide a more standardized product. Crosby focuses on education, to promote quality, and on zero defects, which both Deming and Juran dismiss. And, while Deming and Juran argue for continuous improvement, Crosby argues for heightened awareness or paying attention to what one is doing. Both Deming and Juran argue for statistically grounded quality, while Crosby focuses on influencing human behavior. Deming aims to drive out employee fear of being fired, but Juran argues that a certain amount of fear is necessary, while Crosby redirects the focus from "fear" to paying attention. The views of Deming and Crosby are polar opposites as to where poor quality originates. Deming

Table 4-1
THE APPROACHES OF DEMING, JURAN, AND CROSBY

Deming	Juran	Crosby
continuous training	continuous training	education
zero defects not good	zero defects not good	zero defects are good
continuous improvement	continuous improvement	increased attention
quality system rooted in statistics	statistics are very important	quality rooted in human behavior
top management involvement	top management involvement	top management involvement
get rid of employee fear	a certain level of fear is desirable	promote paying attention
focus on the organizational system	"unknown"	focus on the management system
this system will not fit in present system	this system will fit in present system	this system will fit in present system
management is the root of quality problems	management is the root of problems	workers are key to problems

sees it in the operational system, and Crosby in the managerial system. While Deming's quality system requires a total deconstruction of the current operations system and establishing a new one, Juran and Crosby's quality systems are intended to fit into the existing operations system. And, finally, Deming and Juran see the lack of quality as rooted in management; for example, employees not having good enough equipment to do quality work. Crosby focuses more on the individual worker responsibility.

I think that each of these individuals is right, but partially. What is needed is an integration of the three views, taking the best of each and combining them.

There are three core principles in TQM (Creech, 1994):

1. A customer focus
2. Participation and teamwork
3. Continuous improvement and learning.

Let's look at each of these principles in detail.

Customer Focus

Customer focus is a key aspect of TQM, particularly in meeting or, better, exceeding a customer's quality expectations. From the TQM perspective, the customer is the principal judge of quality. And, while many companies focus primarily on product reliability and its fitness for use, quality, as perceived by a customer—subjective, as well as intersubjective—is important. To demonstrate this point, let us take an example where one would think the objective domain was the most important aspect—a surgical skin-prepping product that must demonstrate antimicrobial efficacy in order to be sold under current Food and Drug Administration requirements. This will also illustrate how practical and effective a quadrant perspective can be.

The intense levels of competition present in the topical antimicrobial market, as well as the ever-tightening Food and Drug Administration's (FDA) product performance standards, demand that antimicrobial soap and detergent manufacturers produce products that meet certain requirements. For purposes of the FDA, these requirements basically are a matter of antimicrobial effectiveness. The market, however, imposes additional requirements. But just what are the market requirements? Beyond antimicrobial effectiveness, they include such factors as low skin irritation, ease of use, good aesthetics, and various other attributes. If all of these have been addressed by the company, the product probably has been developed with concern and competence. But, too often, manufacturers ignore many of these important factors and merely get a product to market to compete with other brands, an approach that frequently fails; the product never really is accepted in the market. Because the goal is to introduce products into the market that will be successful, manufacturers are wise to develop a product from a multi-dimensional perspective, that of the quadrant perspective.

Let us look at the quadrant model in greater detail.

Social Requirements. In this example, social requirements include conforming to the standards of regulating agencies such as the FDA, the Federal Trade Commission (FTC), and the Environmental Protection Agency (EPA), as well as the rules, laws, and regulations they enforce. Before designing a product, it is critical to understand the current legal regulations governing the product, its components and their levels, as well as product stability and toxicological concerns. For example, a New Drug Application (NDA) is required to market a regulated drug product. For over-the-counter (OTC) products, the active drug and its level must be within allowable ranges. Additionally, the FDA's Tentative Final Monograph (TFM) for OTC products, or the "to be determined" requirements of the Cosmetic, Toiletry, and Fragrance Association (CTFA) and the Soap and Detergent Association (SDA) must be addressed.

Cultural Requirements. Cultural requirements are important but often ignored. Cultural and subcultural considerations include shared values, beliefs, goals, and the worldviews of a society or subgroup of society. Shared values such as *perceived* antimicrobial "effectiveness" have great influence on consumers. These values, as we have stated, are generally of two types: manifest and latent. Manifest (surface) values are those of which the consumer is conscious. For example, a consumer buys an antimicrobial soap to be "cleaner" than would be possible using a non-antimicrobial soap. But deeper and more fundamental values are also present. These are referred to as latent values, of which the consumer is unconscious. In this case, "cleaner" may mean to the consumer such things as being accepted, valued, loved, and worthwhile as a person, spouse, and/or parent.

Most manifest and latent values we share as a culture are magnified by manufacturers' advertising campaigns (Maslow, 1954).

The consumer will be motivated by both the manifest and latent values. For example, if a homemaker perceives that she or he is taking better care of the children by having them use antimicrobial soaps (manifest value), and if she or he feels more valuable, more loved, and/or more needed by his or her family, etc. (latent value), the homemaker will be motivated to purchase the product.

Finally, much of what consumers believe to be true is not grounded in objective reality (Kelly, 1955). Most of these beliefs are formed from their interpretation of mass media reports, opinions of others, and explanations of phenomena from various authorities (Koestler, 1976; Hershey, Blanchard & Johnson, 1996).

Personal Objective Attributes. These include the physical components of a product—its application, its antimicrobial actions, or its irritating effects on the skin or in the environment (e.g., staining clothing, gowns, and bedding). It is important that products be designed with the individual in mind (Albaurn, et al., 1994). Hence, products must be easy to use and to open, if in a container, and they must be effective for their intended use (e.g., food servers, home consumers, medical personnel, and surgical personnel).

Personal Subjective Attributes. This category includes one's personal interpretation of cultural and subcultural "worldviews." Relative to antimicrobials, these include, for example, subjective likes and dislikes of characteristics such as the fragrance and feel of the product, the perceived "quality" of the product, and other aesthetic considerations (Wilber, 2000a). As with cultural attributes, there are manifest and latent values in this category. Hence, if one likes the springtime fragrance of a consumer bodywash product (manifest), the latent or deeper value may be that it makes one feel younger and, therefore, more physically attractive and desirable as a person.

These four attribute categories are presented in quadrant form (Figure 4-3) (Fromm, 1968; May, 1977; Walsh, 1984). Notice that each quadrant interacts and is interdependent with the other three quadrants. For example, cultural values influence personal values, and vice-versa. Likewise, cultural and personal values influence behavior and behavior influences values.

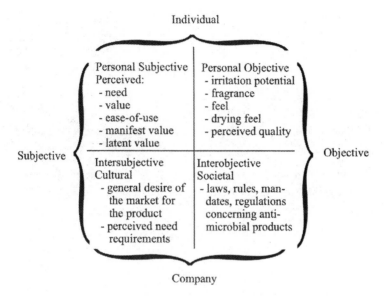

Figure 4-3. Quadrant Model of Attribute Categories

Participation and Teamwork

In TQM, the quality process does not just flow downward, but also upward. A quality issue can be flagged by a manager or a line-assembly person. Employees, when allowed to participate—both individually and in teams—in decisions that affect their jobs and customer value can make substantial contributions to quality. And, training employees to think creatively and "out of the box" helps to develop trust and loyalty. Empowering employees to make decisions that increase quality, without the cumbersome bureaucratic rules, demonstrates high levels of employee trust. Additionally, the system must provide for recognition of individual and team accomplishments (Creech, 1994).

Teamwork is absolutely essential. The use of self-managed teams has become very popular in the United States. This type of structure, combining teamwork with empowerment, is highly effective in getting employees involved.

An important type of team, conceptualized in TQM, is a cross-functional one to which tasks are assigned as a team. Such a team is not composed of members from the same department or area of specialization, but instead, it is cross- or inter-departmental. In an engineering firm, the team, instead of being composed solely of engineers, may contain a member from sales, one from the business group, one from quality assurance, and one from engineering. This tends to break down the artificial barriers often erected by departments, resulting in departitioning of group clusters that do not communicate with other departments, a process critical to the success of the entire firm. Such partitioning often is very problematic for companies. For example, if engineering designs a new product, and the vast majority of this development process is retained within that department, huge errors can occur, such as it not being cost effective or what consumers want. Additionally, it may be flawed in design, without quality being built into the product. Cross-functional teams can avoid such errors in one step.

Continuous Improvement and Learning

In TQM, the concept of continuous improvement is important (Deming, 1982). Continuous quality improvement occurs both in small increments and in what Juran terms breakthroughs—large, rapid improvements. Quality improvements result in value enhancements for customers through new and improved products and services, error, defect and waste reduction, improved productivity and efficiency in the use of all resources, and improved customer responsiveness.

Learning also plays an important role in TQM. Learning is often usefully defined as a positive adaptation to change, leading to new goals and approaches. Learning takes place in the constant iterative comparison of applications and their results. This is generally facilitated via focus stages:

1. Planning
2. Execution of the plan
3. Assessment of the results
4. Revision of the plan based upon results.

Concluding Remarks

Company-individual relational policy has customarily been the job of the CEO, as well as the human resource (HR) group. Unfortunately, most of the effort of today's CEOs and human resource groups is focused solely at the lower right quadrant level (corporate profit, expenses, costs, growth, and prevention of a lawsuit). Employees of many large firms have never even seen the CEO. Moreover, many experienced CEOs who unconsciously understand the value of corporate culture feel they cannot control it, that other firms are worse, or that it takes too much time (Paulson, 2001). But there is a heavy price to pay, often overlooked. It is much like failing to maintain mechanical equipment. A company may make a profit, but an inefficient profit.

It is of great value if a CEO truly understands the importance of win-win corporate goals that are, at once, consistent with individual values and imbues the company and its employees with a sense of these goals. If this occurs, employees tend to be more motivated, because their goals and those of the company coincide. To achieve this, however, requires that a CEO evaluate more than bottom-line profits. It requires attending to the development of a positive corporate culture, one where positive corporate words match positive corporate actions. This often is a challenging task, requiring much patience and skill. But in the end, research shows the results are worthwhile. The firm will be strong, far beyond what the balance sheet shows—and that will be important in the coming years of increased globalization.

The final structure at the employee-company level is depicted in Figure 4-4.

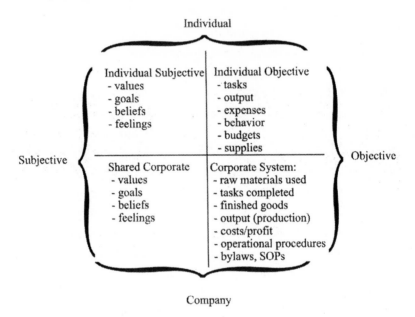

Individual

Individual Subjective
- values
- goals
- beliefs
- feelings

Individual Objective
- tasks
- output
- expenses
- behavior
- budgets
- supplies

Subjective

Objective

Shared Corporate
- values
- goals
- beliefs
- feelings

Corporate System:
- raw materials used
- tasks completed
- finished goods
- output (production)
- costs/profit
- operational procedures
- bylaws, SOPs

Company

Figure 4-4. Employee-Company Structure

CHAPTER 5

Individual-Industry Level

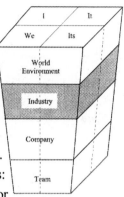

At the level of the individual relative to the industry, the focus is on enabling the company to successfully compete against other firms for market share. This requires a strategy. Strategy—marketing and competitive—is the primary focus at this level. Strategies generally follow one of two courses: 1) adding unique value to a product or service, or 2) offering the goods or services at low cost. Let us now examine each quadrant to understand its place in strategy.

Personal Subjective

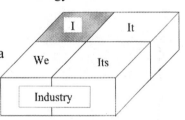

Formulating and implementing a strategy is critical to the long-term sustained success of a business. In order to formulate one, the strategist needs to have a unique view of the playing field. No doubt, a certain number of effective strategists operate at the formal operations level of cognition. That is, they can think about thinking, can conceive a hypothetical situation and cognitively construct a logical outcome. But to excel as a strategist, it is desirable not only to operate within one's corporate logic system, but also simultaneously be able to operate in other business logic systems (Sinnott, 1998). One must be able to act on multiple systems (Commons, et al., 1990). With this ability, one can evaluate and compare multiple systems to select the best one relative to a specific situation, or select aspects from several and integrate them. And, at this level, a person can perceive that systems problems have multiple systems solutions and can select what is "best" from a multiple of systems perspectives to provide integrated solutions.

In order to select a course of action, when one's view of the "playing field" is not clear, intuition can be valuable, particularly when it is grounded in experience (Agor, 1986). Usually, there is an intuitive component in the formulation of successful strategies. Intuition is not "flying by the seat of one's pants;" instead, it relies on many of the same unconscious, psychological mechanisms used by a skilled physician or a chess master. Generally, a person retains a huge amount of unconscious memory, acquired by training and experience that can be drawn upon and applied successfully by those willing to develop intuition as a valid way of knowing. The intuition I am discussing is not emotion, so it is not subject to psychological projections. Rather, it is a level of mental awareness sometimes referred to as "inner vision."

Henry Mintzberg has suggested that strategists should have well-developed right-brain thinking patterns, so as to see the big picture. This implies a relational, holistic use of information—synthesis, rather than analysis. Many executives are adept at intuitive reasoning, and it is what they are doing when they say they "know at the gut level" (Agor, 1984). Intuition appears to be such an important tool that it has been described as the "skill" that separates the executive from managers. In some arenas, the litmus test for executives is the ability to distill tangible and intangible factors— to see the forest *and* the trees, without getting lost in either. Routinely, executives must make strategic decisions in anticipation of future events that are unclear. For this to occur successfully, they must have foresight, the perceptiveness to identify the core concerns, and the ability to allocate resources flexibly in order to cultivate and capitalize on emerging strategic opportunities.

One's intuition is like a muscle. To work well, it must be strengthened through use. Although certain aspects of intuition probably can be taught, most people who have it seem to develop their intuitive abilities naturally through direct experience. Intuition draws on our subconscious mental processes and incorporates previous experiences to foster new insights. Psychologists tell us that one effective way to tap into intuition is to incubate ideas (Barasch, 2000). Incubation is a process of giving free rein to the subconscious to mull over a situation in the presence of the relevant, known facts. Often, an "aha!" experience will result from this, where one perceives the situation clearly and knows, or rather intuits, what to do.

The personal subjective domain is also the arena where one must form one's personal values. Strategy formulation often is practiced as if values and ethics are secondary. It is well known that individuals are able to neglect their values of right and wrong in a group, because group dynamics are such that one feels little personal responsibility for the group's actions (Fadiman & Frager, 2002; Newman, 1997). Group dynamics, in part, explain why atrocities against minority groups were repeatedly overlooked by solid citizens in Nazi-occupied territories during World War II. And these dynamics are still operative in perhaps the majority of businesses today. For example, it was known to certain executives that the Firestone tire design was flawed and led to a number of deaths. Yet, no one at the executive level at Firestone stood up and said, "No, I will not be a part of the fraudulent practice of concealing a known safety problem." This is not because these individuals are inherently bad. Instead, no one said anything because no one felt personally responsible. At a lower level of personal moral development, that is to be expected. But at the executive level, personal ethical responsibility must be developed. From a growth perspective of moral development, men and women tend to move through three general stages: preconventional (egocentric), conventional (sociocentric), and postconventional (world-centric). Men tend to progress through these stages based more on judgments of rights and justice, and women tend to negotiate these stages based on care and concern (Gilligan, 1982). Unfortunately, the Firestone situation was controlled by executives who were not beyond the preconventional level.

Additionally, when a person is able to dissociate personal responsibility from business, one can perform despicable acts that one would not ordinarily perform. For example, business executives, and particularly attorneys, whom I have questioned pointedly about personal responsibility in their business dealings, often state, "it is business, and I can't become emotionally attached," or something substantively the same (Gardner, et al., 2001). Some executives rationalize that they ignore ethical responsibility because their competitors do. A substantial number fantasize they are analogous to a Samurai warrior involved in war, where every action is fair. Interestingly, most of those whom I have interviewed avoided the draft during the Vietnam War; it's also worth noting that being identified with the Samurai warrior is a grand fiction (Paulson, 1994).

What must be exemplified in business management is responsibility and a sense of fair play—in a word, ethics. Actually developing a superior product or service, learning how to deal with people through win-win interactions, and treating others fairly and with compassion are things essential to succeeding in the global market over the long haul. The sense of fair play is based in compassion and acknowledges, at a fundamental level, that we are all brothers and sisters, an ethical view that is all-inclusive. The pursuit of moral development in business can make a huge, positive difference (Hunter, 2000). But it will take a few who are not afraid to step up to the plate.

Personal Objective

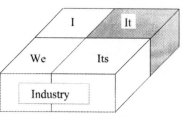

The personal objective domain consists of carrying out the tasks planned in the strategy. We have just discussed several aspects of the personal subjective dimension that are as important as the objective aspects of actually carrying out the plan. In this era of high-speed, low-cost microcomputers, an individual can vastly augment his or her abilities to carry out strategy.

In becoming ever more competitive to keep up with global trends, a strategist will need to provide quality products or services, while keeping prices down. Applications such as linear programming—probably better called linear modeling—can provide the strategist a clear plan for maximization of profits (or minimization of costs) from a firm's existing product/service mix, based upon the actual market situation. Then, based on the quantitative model's output and a sensitivity analysis (evaluating how robust the quantitative model's solution data are, relative to unforeseen changes in product or service demands, as well as costs, labor, and supply), one can determine how applicable the model is in the real world (Render & Stair, 2000).

Lower Quadrants

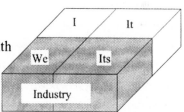

Companies generally compete with other companies that offer similar goods and services to consumers. If there is no recognized advantage of one product or service over another, given ready availability of the product/service, the *cheaper* ones will be in greater demand. A common approach to preventing this—competition focused mainly on price—is to add "value." That is, add recognizably valuable attributes to the basic product or service so as to differentiate it from one's competitors. Given the buyer recognizes increased value, the product/service can be sold at a higher price. But, there are only so many ways to add value and, eventually, the market contains clusters of "differentiated" products/services, but within each cluster the products/services are very similar. Here, again, price becomes the main issue within the clusters. Bartlett and Ghosshal (1992) have argued that competition has become so intense that, to be successful, firms must use both product/service differentiation and low-cost pricing strategies to be competitive, particularly in international markets.

Strategic management, which includes strategic marketing in this work, is generally thought of as an objective endeavor, linking the company to the industry, but that is not entirely so. Both subjective and intersubjective domains play key roles in determining an effective strategy and carrying it out. For example, buyers (particularly other businesses) like to meet seller company personnel to see "faces." Intersubjective bonding between members in these groups is critical, because an ongoing interpersonal relationship is necessary. The maxim "companies do not do business with companies, but with people" is true. And, likewise, a large proportion of strategy formulation is not only the outcome of a strategist's personal cognitive abilities, but also his or her interactions among other strategists, managers, and marketing personnel within the company.

It must also be recognized that the types of information used to formulate the strategy are, themselves, grounded in shared interpersonal concepts—e.g., amortization methods, financial interpretations, procedures for computing the return on investments, and marketing data—all of which invariably magnify certain business aspects and minimize others. Additionally, most strategies—operational or marketing—are not based on unbiased data, but on biased data, stemming from "beliefs" assumed to be "facts," partial knowledge presented as the total picture of reality, and models assumed to portray reality.

In the process of formulating business strategy, there are a number of perspectives and viewing frames from which to evaluate them. However, each perspective provides a view that argues for its own relative validity, as well as the invalidity of the other views. Most business strategists believe that their view is the *true* picture of "the situation," but not surprisingly, other corporate strategists in the same market have differing views, which they consider true (Hamel & Prahalad, 1994). Recall that, at a postformal level of thinking, multiple views of reality are the norm. So each of these views, while being true, is not the whole truth. It is a part of a larger truth.

Let us now turn our attention to some actual strategic perspectives widely used today.

Positioning Perspective

By far the most popular has been called the "Positioning Perspective," championed by a Harvard Business School professor, Michael Porter (1980; 1985; 1990). Yet, we need to keep in mind that there are other valuable strategic perspectives, such as the "Design" and "Planning" views, and the negotiations-centered view, used to form strategic alliances. The "Learning Perspective" is also valuable and, not to be omitted is the "Entrepreneurial Perspective," often providing a fresh way of "seeing." Psychological and epistemological views[1] also have an important place in strategy; their contribution is sometimes referred to as the "Cognitive Perspective." There are also "Cultural" and "Systems" views we will discuss. Although each of these views provides a unique picture of reality, it will certainly be valuable to integrate these perspectives, so as to provide not only a more complete view of reality, but a more complete way of dealing with it.

Let us begin with Michael Porter's Positioning Perspective. For

Porter, strategy is the process of positioning the company within the industry's environment to capitalize on the company's strengths and protect its weaknesses (1985). And, as Porter points out, the industry's structure has a strong influence in determining how companies position themselves. The competitive structure of an industry is rooted in the underlying economic structure, which involves, too, the relationship of individual to the environment, which I discuss in the next chapter. Porter's competitive view, in a given industry, is determined by five basic forces (Figure 5-1).

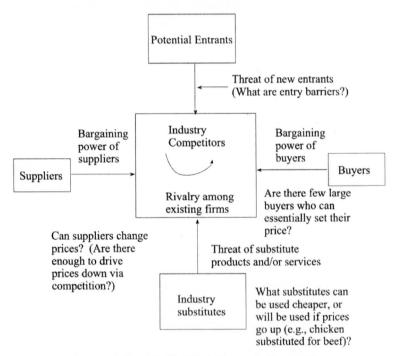

Figure 5-1. Porter's Five Basic Forces in Competition

Figure 5-1 shows that new entrants into an industry bring new capacities to compete for the same markets, often supported by substantial resources (Hitt, et al., 1999; Montgomery & Porter, 1991). To a large degree, the actual threat of new entrants into an industry depends upon the "entry barriers" presented by existing competitors and the retaliation of these competitors on new entrants. If the barriers are high (e.g., difficult to surmount in time, technology, and money) and/or the reaction to new entrants by current competitors is strong, then the threat of entry by new competitors into a particular industry is low. Rivalry among existing firms, another force, takes place in the industry when firms jockey for market position via price leadership, advertising campaigns, new product launches, increasing customer services, and extended product/service warranties. Competitive pressure exists from substitute products/services that limit the potential returns of competitors in an industry by placing a price ceiling on goods and services (Hill & Jones, 1998; Mintzberg, et al., 1998). For example, if chicken prices increase, beef, pork, or fish may be substituted, keeping the chicken price at a specific ceiling range.

Buyers can have a strong influence on competitors if they have bargaining power within an industry to demand more services or higher-quality services from suppliers or to pit one supplier against another in pricing. Suppliers also can also attain power over competitors within an industry, particularly when there are few suppliers. For example, by increasing prices, reducing quality, and the like, a supplier can leverage a competitor out of the market.

According to Porter, these five factors are the main forces driving industrial competition. Most business strategists agree that to compete successfully, a firm must have contingencies to deal with these five forces, as well as be able to compete in terms of:
1. Pricing strategy (cheapest)
2. Differentiation strategy (increased value, or as Porter suggests, increasing the value chain length as cheaply as possible)
3. Focus strategy (this leads to focused price leadership and differentiation, aimed at different niche markets.)

Porter's Positioning Perspective strategy is exceedingly valuable, particularly for large corporate manufacturing entities. However, it does have several weaknesses. In particular, its strategic view is narrow, being centered in economics, which is Porter's expertise. And both subjective and intersubjective domains of human existence are totally ignored, thus leaving the model blind to important fluctuations in cultural values, cultural meaning, and cultural goals, for example. Porter seems to intuit the importance of this, while never articulating it. Although he acknowledges that subjective/intersubjective domains are important, they are not identified specifically, nor employed as strategic goals.[2] Porter's view is also heavily weighted toward large business dynamics and has been criticized as "an ivory tower" approach. For example, Lowendahl argues that Positioning strategy is not especially useful in small professional firms, such as engineering or scientific consultant groups, and the like (Lowendahl, 1997).

Design Perspective

Case studies are a core teaching device in most MBA programs, and case studies are a main component of the Design Perspective. Strategically, from a "design" point of view, one tries to fit or match a firm's resource capabilities to the opportunities available in a particular industry. This is accomplished via a "SWOT" analysis.[3] That is, the *strengths* and *weaknesses* of one's organization, an internal component, are identified, as are the *opportunities* and *threats* in the industry—an external component. The strengths of an organization and the opportunities of an industry are matched and exploited. The weaknesses of a firm are protected and the threats of an industry avoided. Industry opportunity is usually the main factor. If no opportunity exists, the others are moot points. Design Perspective strategists continually scan for industrial opportunities that match a company's core competencies well. Additionally, they are also alert for opportunities that do not exactly match company core competencies, but, with just a few minor changes, can.

The Design Perspective is an objective domain-centered strategic system that ignores, for the most part, both subjective and intersubjective reality. Hence, human factors are ignored, except for what they can do to increase production or sales capacity. It should be understood, then, that the Design Perspective, like the Positioning Perspective, is blind to a strategist's personal influences—values, desires, ethics, beliefs—as well as company-shared intersubjective influences on the input and output of information, and on the strategic planning process itself. This blinded view can be disastrous, indeed.

Take, for example, the Vietnam War, which was conducted using a Design Strategy Perspective. Robert McNamara, one of Harvard's most famous MBA graduates, and his staff members carefully assessed and analyzed the "objective situation" in Vietnam. With tons of bombs dropping daily on enemy territory in both North and South Vietnam, and with more than a half-million United States military troops in South Vietnam, the United States still lost that war. The United States had a military organization far superior to that of North Vietnam, which, for practical purposes, had virtually no air power, no naval power, poor equipment, no mechanized infantry, and had suffered at least a 20:1 kill ratio in America's favor. Still the war was lost, mainly because U.S. strategists were blind to the significance of North Vietnam's superiority in culturally shared beliefs, values, and goals, and the enormous advantage of focus and determination these provided them to fight on. U.S. strategists also failed to consider the effects of the United States' cultural rejection of the war. Needless to say, applying the Design Perspective to winning in Vietnam was an utter fiasco.

Another concern with the Design Perspective is that it is difficult to measure the actual collected data in terms of accuracy and precision to validate the SWOT analysis portrayal of objective business reality. This is partly because subjective personal and intersubjective biases (perceived values, goals, beliefs, and so on) interfere with the acquisition of purely objective data and interpretation of their meaning. All too often, the presumed objective data, assumed to be without error, are actually interpretations of other interpretations. And, too, a SWOT analysis often is biased by corporate politics and individuals trying to advance their interests, instead of determining "what is."

Planning Perspective

The Planning Perspective, more popular several decades ago, is rooted in the Design Perspective but is expanded in scope to the nth degree of detail, delineating steps, providing charts and checklists, setting objectives, and elaborating on budgets and operating plans for the corporate, business, functional, and operational levels. However, a benefit of the Planning Perspective is that a plan (marketing and operational) is not only drafted in operational detail, but also is implemented at various organization levels, between teams (divisions, sections, etc.) and among individuals (Montgomery & Porter, 1991). This is an important practical aspect, because research shows that a strategy not carefully laid out throughout the firm is never fully implemented. The Planning Perspective does this (Hill & Jones, 1998).

But this is not all it does. It also is responsible for the use of "scenario" contingency planning and modeling. In this process, various "what if" situations are presented, and strategists formulate a set of contingency plans to deal successfully with the "what if" situations (Fahey & Randall, 1998).

A drawback with the Planning Perspective is that the construction process frequently becomes overly bureaucratic, favoring procedures over practicality. Additionally, it is expensive, time consuming, and, even when implemented, it is of limited realized value to the firm, often because the assumption that data collected are both objective and complete is not true. As many human and empirical scientists state, however, a detached, objective perspective on reality, as assumed under the Planning Perspective, is not possible. One does not have a clear view of reality; one has a socially, culturally, and personally constructed view of reality (Searle, 1995). Each strategy formulator unconsciously introduces biases (e.g., view points, concepts, and interpretations), distorting the model's representation of reality. Additionally, the Planning Perspective ignores subjective and intersubjective interactions (e.g., group dynamics), despite the planning process itself being mainly an intersubjective one.

Negotiation Perspective

This perspective draws heavily on interpersonal communication theory, psychology, and rhetoric, and is grounded in the intersubjective domain of shared concepts, beliefs, and meaning, as well as on components of the personal subjective domain, such as worldview, beliefs, wants, and meaning (Brooks & Odiorne, 1984). Yet the main thrust is undoubtedly in the objective domain. The primary tool in the Negotiation Perspective has been convincing others to accept a particular solution by means of argumentation, pressure, persuasion, subtle intimidation, staging, stalling, leveraging, and cohesion (Mintzberg, et al., 1998). Needless to say, this caused much distrust in the industry and is not the type of negotiation to which I am referring. The negotiation process has matured over the decades; the goal is no longer to win at the expense of the other side, but to create a win-win solution, one that is desired by both sides. This type of negotiation process focuses on mutual interests, not just self-interests (Illich, 1973). Hence, the process entails the invention of new, creative solution options for mutual gain.

Because the ultimate goal resides generally in the objective domain, the criteria for evaluating the terms of the negotiated agreement must also be objective. The Negotiation Perspective recognizes companies as being composed of humans who have needs, motivations, desires, and aspirations. If these needs can be discovered and then met in the larger perspective, the desired outcome can be achieved.

There is little doubt of the tremendous positive value of the Negotiation Perspective, if applied open-handedly. And from a strategic perspective, inter-company alliances are becoming ever more important, the joining of forces to compete more successfully in the global environment. Such competitive alliances, in that they increase the allies' position power and resource power, are often easier to control than had one firm developed the partners' capabilities by itself. However, achieving a strong and durable strategic alliance requires a good professional business fit—objective, intersubjective, and personal subjective—among those involved. And, too, allied companies must have each other's best interests at the fore and act accordingly, not only on the surface, but at deeper levels, too.

Learning Perspective

The Learning Perspective provides another unique approach to management strategy and is based on the acknowledged fact that it takes time to become not just good, but proficient at producing a company's core goods and services (Oster, 1999). Over time, as a company learns how to compete in the marketplace, it becomes progressively better because of its ability to learn or acquire knowledge and apply that knowledge to competing in the world (Banathy, 1996).

The Learning Perspective addresses an aspect that no other perspective does—the emergent aspect—that of continually transcending its present limits. And often, this poised receptivity enables a firm to acquire valuable knowledge it was not intending to acquire. This is also a phenomenon valued in science, giving rise to the aphorism "chance favors the prepared mind." For example, the discovery of the "Big Bang" by Bell Laboratory personnel was precipitated by a chance mistake, realized subsequently as a hugely important "find." Fleming's accidental discovery that the common laboratory mold contaminant *Penicillium* killed bacteria led through further experimentation to the development of antibiotics immensely valuable in treating infectious diseases. Firestone's discovery that heating rubber makes it resistant to wear was behind the evolution of modern tire manufacturing.

The Learning Perspective is a continuous developmental process. A company can actively support learning quickly and decrease its time on the learning curve by integrating emergent knowledge with experience. A well-known champion of this approach is Peter Senge (1990) and his work with the "learning companies." Another advocate is Chris Argyris (1982; 1992; 1993) through his work with group learning. The Learning Perspective acknowledges that the intersubjective and subjective domains of existence are important, but only insofar as they increase objective efficiency, productivity, and performance. Yet, for beneficial learning to occur, the subjective and intersubjective domains must be appreciated more fully. Personal and group goals, expectations, output, and learning are strongly rooted in intersubjective and subjective values, goals, meaning, direction, and purpose. Learning, as education specialists tell us, does not emerge in a vacuum (Borg & Gall, 1989).

A firm's culture must support the learning process. Mistakes are made that provide valuable knowledge as to what to avoid. When mistakes are not permissible and *perfection is required*, the open-mindedness that enhances learning is missing. No further learning—particularly the accelerated kind—can occur.

That core competencies are those a firm has *learned* to do, through trial and error, very efficiently and uniquely, is Hamel and Prahalad's (1994) contribution to the Learning Perspective concept. Core competencies are acquired through the organization's unique ability to provide value to customers over a long period of time. In successful companies, there are usually three to four core competencies that are pivotal. Not all of a firm's capabilities provide the potential for true competitive advantage. The value of capabilities is relative to industry demand. For capabilities to be valuable, they must enable a firm to exploit current opportunities or neutralize current threats in the industrial environment. Valuable capabilities are generally unique to a firm; they are rarely external attributes, but rather are the application of firm-specific knowledge and, therefore, not easily imitated.

Given these criteria are met, a company has a competitive advantage over rivals. Just how competencies are applied by a firm to generate profit are also a focus of Learning Perspective because this, too, is learned.

Entrepreneurial Perspective

The Entrepreneurial Perspective is a popular area of focus, presented in books, as "manifesting a new vision," putting one's "heart and soul into the business," or "shaking up the business" (Kao, 1989). While some of the approaches are over-simplified, many are useful, particularly in that the entrepreneurial vision provides the markets with many of its new products and new jobs, launches creative work environments, and invents new ways of doing business. Far from being easy, Entrepreneurial Perspective strategies require consistent, persistent effort. An entrepreneur, by definition, must go it alone. And, unlike an established business, an entrepreneur usually does not have an established corporate culture promoting stability and predictability within the organization. The culture must, instead, be established from the ground up. The entrepreneur is continually provided advice that is often contradictory concerning actions and pursuits that will, and will not, work. Hence, she or he must be able not only to think but also act independently, knowing that she or he may be wrong. Entrepreneurs, then, must take unpredictable risks that, not surprisingly, attract stockholders who want immediate double-digit returns on their investments and the constant reassurance of low-risk decisions.

Even with the stresses, most entrepreneurs favor that lifestyle to that of working for someone else (Kelley, 1985); they like the concept of building businesses that exploit profitable niches the larger companies ignore. Additionally, the entrepreneur has much more freedom to try out new things than do employees of an established firm. The entrepreneur can heavily influence the corporate culture and, in fact, establish it with his or her policies and actions. Perhaps one of the first groups who will recognize the value of the Integral Business Perspective will be the entrepreneurs. This is because they are not afraid to try new things and configure them to work. They understand the value of interpersonal relations, leadership, and risk-taking. They have tolerance for ambiguity, spend time understanding themselves subjectively, are flexible, and are grounded in objective reality.

The entrepreneur, to be successful, is forced to apply and blend intuition, knowledge, and mature judgment to birth a unique perspective concerning his or her company relative to the industry. But the entrepreneur needs more than vision. Application of the vision is necessary, or no tangible accomplishments would occur. Typically, then, a core asset of entrepreneurs is that they are "movers and shakers." They get things done.

As Peter Drucker (1985) has argued, an entrepreneur is an economic risk-taker, a common phenomenon in all business at this time, so we all are entrepreneurs, whether we like it or not. The Entrepreneurial Perspective incorporates both an active and a passive search for new opportunity. When opportunity is discovered, the entrepreneurial view enables creation of strategies to take action quickly. A weakness of this view, however, is its blindness to other views. Another is that individuals focused in this view have trouble articulating what they know and how they know, which unfortunately inhibits the transfer of valuable knowledge. This also hampers the firm, in that the entrepreneurial view, being so flexible, is often not consistent enough for long-term planning (Peters, 1987).

Of all the strategic perspectives discussed, the entrepreneurial one is closest to being all-quadrant. Yet, a common problem is that many entrepreneurial companies have difficulty developing beyond the Entrepreneurial Perspective when it is no longer useful. That is, as the company grows over time, the absence of formal structure and process, seemingly so valuable in the past, becomes a detriment. At some time, if a company is to survive over the long haul, it must incorporate standard operating procedures, rules, and regulations to support smooth transitions as the company expands in size.

Cognitive Perspective

This strategic perspective is particularly valuable for some very important criticisms to strategic planning that it provides, e.g., that much planning and decision-making applied to business strategy is based upon data assumed to be true that are actually not (Polkinghorne, 1983). Upon investigation, research has shown that the data thought to be true frequently are, in fact, beliefs about beliefs, interpretations of other individuals' concepts, and partial truths interpreted as whole truths (Paulson, 2001). For example, in conducting a SWOT analysis, how does one really *know* that the opportunities and threats of the industry, as well as the strengths and weaknesses of the company, are true? And, if true, to what degree—partially true or all-encompassingly true? How much does a particular SWOT analysis rely on interpretations, as opposed to data collected in an unbiased manner based on a verified epistemology, or even a valid hermeneutical procedure? (Epistemology is the study of how one can be sure that information is true, instead of merely believing information is true. Hermeneutics is the study of how data are interpreted.)

Hence, the cognitive view argues for a valid epistemology to assure that data used are true and complete, and the methods used in their collection are valid. It also argues the importance of questioning and challenging data until the data have been demonstrated true, or at least have a high probability of being true. Business decision-makers often deceive themselves by demanding the strategic situation be black and white—no grey. This is particularly true in managerial quantitative analysis, where mathematical models serve to provide an analyst a false sense of security by providing a clear-cut answer that can only be a partial truth, at best. Humans, by nature, want to remove ambiguity to reduce their tension about making a wrong decision, but this opens the door for all sorts of distortions, such as the Hawthorne Effect, the Pygmalion Effect, the John Henry Effect, and even Magical Thinking (Borg & Gall, 1989).

Recall that the Hawthorne Effect, discussed in Chapter 3, occurs when a business group performs to the assumed expectation of the investigator. The Pygmalion Effect occurs when a business analyst or manager has a preconceived perspective of a business group, to which the business then conforms. The John Henry Effect occurs when a business group used as a benchmark perceives this and exceeds its usual level of performance, thereby negating its benchmark value. Magical Thinking describes the assumption of conclusions derived neither logically nor systematically.

Let us look at these phenomena through examples. If a team of strategists evaluates the industry and falls into the Hawthorne Effect, they will interpret the results in a way that reflects what they feel their supervisor wants to see. In a Pygmalion Effect, a supervisor presents his or her perspective on the industry situation, and the group automatically incorporates this view as the truth. A John Henry Effect can occur when a group perceives they are being scrutinized and, as a result, performs its responsibilities far better than is usual. In cases of Magical Thinking, analysts will conclude that the outcome they want will, in fact, occur, despite there being no data to support that conclusion.

Unlike the sciences, in which data are scrupulously collected to assure both their internal and external validity, business data are prone to bias. This is not because business analysts are incompetent, but more often because management needs to see and believe what it wants to see and believe. Because there is so much pressure on them to control the situation, they often are forced to "pretend" they have a control that they do not (Kelly, 1955; Bandura, 1997). And unlike in the sciences, where data are freely given, businesses tend to guard their data and provide it only when it is advantageous, and then, in its best light.

The Cognitive Perspective points out that humans make many decisions based on subjective concerns, sometimes far removed from objective concerns. Then, they rationalize their choices as the logical thing to do. The Cognitive Perspective suggests, finally, that to admit the data may be distorted, incomplete, etc., is far better, strategically, than to pretend it is not. In an important sense, the Cognitive Perspective is the "reality check" that *should* underlie all of the other strategic processes.

Cultural Perspective

The Cultural Perspective utilizes collective group dynamics in strategy development. To a large degree, it is based upon cultural groups working together as a unified team, enhancing the capacity of a firm to get tasks accomplished. From the cultural viewpoint, developing team spirit—*esprit de corps*—engenders an urge to be "number one," the "best," the "most efficient," and so on. An important advantage of this view is that shared convictions can quickly change organizational behavior because the group is motivated by the emotional fuel of participating in something that matters and is larger than the individual.

Much of Tom Peters' work (1987) in "excellence" reflects the Cultural Perspective. In application, it is necessary that executive management be linked with line workers by having executives actually walking around to see first-hand what is happening in the "trenches." Tom Peters' maxim of "management by walking around" was derived from this process. Leaving the executive ivory tower to find out what the employees really think, what problems they really face—and listening to what they have to say—can be enlightening.

Companies that are highly successful—have achieved excellence—are usually dominated by shared, key values (service, quality, going the extra mile, and so on). A critical aspect, however, is that for shared meaning to really influence productivity, it must be shared at a deep level, not just on the surface. A shared, positive deep-level commitment confers a huge competitive advantage (which is how North Vietnam won the war, as I pointed out earlier).

Companies with a strong cultural orientation require mature managers who do not look out just for their own interests, but are able to formulate fair, "win-win" dynamics. This generally is a long process requiring corporate culture stability, based on earned interpersonal trust between management and labor. Not surprisingly, effective implementation of the Cultural Perspective is rare, as are companies displaying true excellence.

One overshadowing problem with the Cultural Perspective,

however, is that it tends to ignore the benefits of planning, steady persistent action, and the application of methodical business procedures to achieve desired goals. Instead, it is more like air leaving a balloon, forceful and fast at first, then winding down and finally petering out.

Systems Perspective

Systems practices, particularly applied to management, have evolved during the twentieth century, spanning fields as diverse as the physical, medical, and social sciences, as well as engineering and business (Bertalanffy, 1968; Senge, 1990; Sterman, 2000). Systems management practices incorporate many of the tools of engineering, for example, feedback interrelationships found in cybernetics, and the concept of servo-mechanics found in mechanical engineering.

The main focus of the Systems Perspective applied to strategy is the industry environment itself. In this view, the firm is subordinate to the environment; hence, both leadership style and organizational strategic practice must be adaptive to the external industrial environment in which the company exists. This situation is much like an ecological situation in which species of organisms fill niches within the constraints of the environment. A firm is also viewed as needing to fill a niche, if it is to survive. The firm must compete for niche expansion, just as an anemone group competes for a larger part of the rock it occupies, and must do so successfully, or become extinct through competition.

Additionally, a systems view of strategy requires the understanding of one's firm in the context of the industry. Systems management does not approach strategy as mere sets of linear cause-and-effect relationships; instead, it views strategy as a continuous system of interdependent relationships (Wilber, 2000a; 2000b). Let us look at an example.

Suppose there are two organizations, A and B, that compete against one another through price-reduction strategies. Company A sees Company B drop its prices, so it does the same. Company B, seeing Company A drop its prices, drops its prices.

Company A perceives the situation this way:

Company B⎯⎯→ Threat to ⎯⎯→ Company A
drops prices   Company A   must drop prices

Company B perceives the situation precisely in reverse:

Company A⎯⎯→ Threat to ⎯⎯→ Company B
drops prices   Company B   must drop prices

While both perspectives are true, they are only partially true. They illustrate a linear cause-and-effect perspective, which is not how the situation is in the "world." A systems strategy perspective, however, provides a "more real" view of the whole situation, leading to a more comprehensive understanding of how the parts within the whole influence and interact with one another (see Figure 5-2).

Systems analysis reveals that the price war is perpetuated by both companies, in that each perceives the other as a threat, without acknowledging their own involvement in, and influence on, the situation.

Systems Perspective promotes a strategic style of seeing objective wholes and parts. It provides the framework for seeing interobjective relationships, rather than isolated phenomena, for seeing patterns and processes of change, rather than static "snapshots."

The systems strategic focus is the *market environment* composed of the entire industry, not just a company—a system of systems, in other words. This is an extremely important area of focus, for it forces the firm to see the larger picture and the firm's relationship to it. And from a systems view, situations that may be valued as "good" at the company level may not be, at this broader

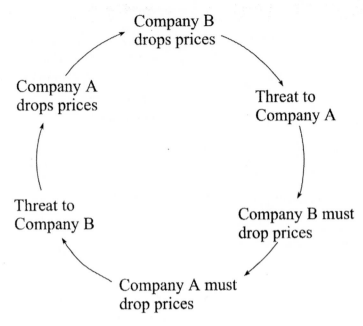

Figure 5-2. Systems Perspective

level. For example, extremely rapid growth, which is much desired by entrepreneurs, investors, etc., is viewed much like cancer—out of control. And it is well known that very few fast-growing firms can exist over the long haul without voluntary limits on growth. Appropriate growth of a company should be achieved at a steady, persistent, and controlled rate, determined by the company's capabilities and its dynamic relationship to the industry (Banathy, 1996).

Although there is much to appreciate in the systems approach, it does tend to ignore the importance of the subjective and inter-subjective domains, as well as the importance of particular components of the specific firm. Once again, then, a specific perspective has its strengths that can be applied to advantage, but weaknesses, too, that argue against strategic tunnel vision.

Other Perspectives

Political action, as in the world at large, is important in strategy. For simplicity, I include the Political Perspective within the Negotiation Perspective. A value in the Political Perspective is that it uses political leverage and political clout to get financing, for example, via government funding. It is also important to acknowledge a strategy of using a "hot" or popular item, to exploit the shared values a group (consumers) places on the item (rock star, author, athlete, etc.), a concept that is really a part of the Cultural Perspective.

The Strategic View Quadrant Model

Based on this overview, let us now characterize these strategic views through the quadrant framework (see Figure 5-3). As we have seen, each view offers valuable contributions to strategy, but is incomplete on its own. To get a more comprehensive approach to strategizing, we need to integrate the views.

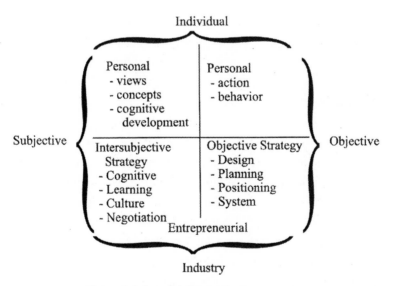

Figure 5-3. Strategic Views Quadrant Model

Integration

Please keep in mind that the purpose of integration is not to be fair to everyone's views, but to make more effective strategy. Each strategy is important in that it presents a different, but valid, view. We are, then, weaving them together to have a competitive advantage, not just to increase the bottom line, but to contribute to humanity.

Notice that each strategic view—except the entrepreneurial view—tends to focus more in one quadrant than in any of the other three (Figure 5-3). So, for a more comprehensive and effective strategic management approach, one that provides strategic intent in not only the objective world, but in the subjective and intersubjective worlds as well, they need to be integrated. This integrated strategic model (Figure 5-4, adapted from Mintzberg, et al., 1998) employs the Entrepreneurial Perspective (innovation, looking for new ways of doing things, new opportunities, risk taking, and creativity) at its leading edge.

So, in an integrated approach, when an operational opportunity is discovered, it is evaluated from the Design Perspective (e.g., SWOT-type analysis). Or, if a strategic alliance looks promising, the Negotiation Perspective may take charge of the strategy. Given an attractive opportunity, the Cognitive Perspective assures that the concepts and data used to evaluate the opportunity are valid and grounded in the environment. If that is satisfactory, the Positioning Perspective of price leadership, differentiation, both, or focused price leadership/differentiation will be engaged, relative to the five forces of competition. When an opportunity is pursued, the Planning Perspective, and its detailed instructions between levels and groups in the firm, is applied. Additionally, various scenarios can be rehearsed to better assure that all the bases are covered. All of this takes place in a cultural atmosphere of shared values within the company, relative to its produced goods and services. And that Cultural Perspective must be a "win-win" one. Finally, from its

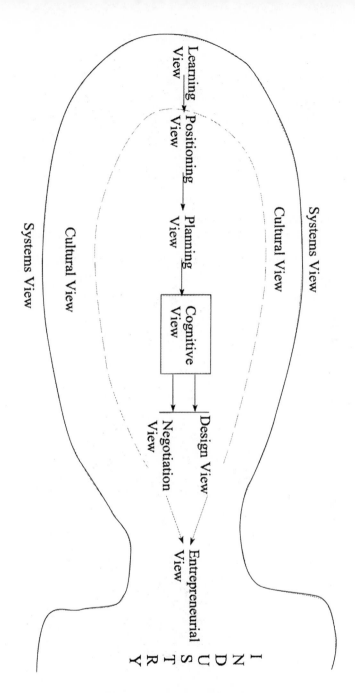

Figure 5-4. Integrated Strategic Views

past operations, the company culture learns from its mistakes, becoming better at what it does and creating a core competency. All of this takes place within the industry environment, which is measured and evaluated from a systems perspective. There is nothing special about the configuration presented in Figure 5-4. It is similar to the fine work of Mintzberg, et al. (1998). Others may find it more useful to reconfigure the perspectives, and that is to be expected. The important point is the knowledge that *all* these views, when integrated, provide an "emergent factor" that adds value beyond the sum of the perspectives. This process enables each firm to take from these perspectives the best for the current need, while never ignoring the others.

CHAPTER 6

Individual-Environmental Level

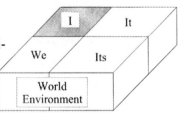

This level, the individual, as she or he relates to the environment at large, is the broadest as well as the most fundamental level. It is fundamental in that it includes the natural environment in which we live, as well as the global human village with its multiple cultures and multiple social practices. It is the broadest level because it encompasses a system-of-systems-of-systems business perspective. Let us examine each quadrant perspective at the broad level to become better oriented.

Personal Subjective

For an individual not only to negotiate, but to excel at negotiating, the environmental domain from a personal perspective, a team perspective, a company perspective, and an industry perspective requires a high degree of personal development and adaptive and integrative ability, particularly in cognitive, moral, and even spiritual developmental lines of intelligence (Barnard, 1968; Newman, 1997). True, developmentally arrested individuals do function successfully at this level, often exceedingly well, looking out for themselves politically and financially, with little care or concern beyond that. But we will not be burdened with this narcissism, particularly after September 11, 2001. We want a broader vision, one in which we truly can be powerful yet compassionate, one in which we do not just take, but contribute, too.

To truly excel at such an advanced level in this perspective requires not only post-formal operational thinking skills, but an ability for post-post-formal operational thinking that enables one to conceptualize in terms of systems of systems of systems (Commons, et al., 1990). At this level (a world-centric perspective), an individual not only interacts directly with teams, the company, the industry, but now, too, with the environment in which the industry is situated. Instead of being caught amongst the multitude of conflicting goals at this level, a person now must hold these in mind, integrating them at a holistically higher (more inclusive) level, the "dialectical process" (Sinnott, 1998). This is a process we have previously discussed, when reducing a three-dimensional cylinder to a two-dimensional view. We get conflicting representations, a circle and a rectangle. This capability, to conceptualize multiple views—political, economic, legal, moral, environmental, and business—is the mark of a truly great human being (Assagioli, 1965).

Openness to new views is obviously necessary at this level, so one can recognize and appreciate the varied cultures, religions, political systems, economic systems, and legal/ethical systems that connect humans into myriad groupings. In fact, all life is valued "as it is" (Smart, 1999). The originator of the middle way (Mahayana) in Buddhism, Nargarjuna argued that clinging to any view as absolute truth leads to suffering. All views are partial, not complete (Murti, 1955; Ramanan, 1975).

Personal Objective

This region represents the actualizing skills necessary to carrying out effective, fair decisions, but it encompasses more than these.

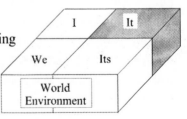

This is the region where one can witness directly the different cultures, religions, political systems, and philosophies, as they are found in the world. Functioning at a high level in this region will require that one come to terms with the inconsistencies between beliefs and behavior found in every culture's systems (Deutsch, 2001). This process often has a shocking impact on an aware observer. One can see, for example, the failings of a democratic society where greater "equality" is granted to the wealthy, and political clout and influence are more important than fairness (Brown, 1997; Harvey, 1990). Such failings are, in no way, missing from non-democratic societies, either. There is truth in social Darwinism, in that those financially and politically stronger will dominate.

At this level, one can distinguish clearly the hypocrisy between words and deeds of broad-sweeping ideals such as fairness and justice for all, collective benefit, and even God's love (Smith, 1997). This is not to condemn these ideas, but to see their shortcomings.

It is with these realizations that one has choices: to act merely for one's own benefit or to act in ways beneficial to all humanity, in spite of apparent absurdity (Kekes, 1995). For example, unless individuals voluntarily prevent themselves from acting only for their sole benefit, the world will pretty much continue on its course of the rich getting richer and the poor getting poorer, a widely obvious source of constant, increasing conflict.

Lower Collective Quadrants

Again, let us examine the lower quadrants together. Individuals, as a whole, making up the environment also have shared beliefs, meaning, goals, aspirations, and values (Maslow, 1954; Fromm, 1968). These are

generally viewed as basic human issues, as well as social issues.

Hence, the environment is viewed in terms of not only consumers, but international governmental rules and regulations, as well as political forces, religious forces, international protective tariffs, macro-economic states, and labor availability. Generally, social/cultural factors addressed at the environmental level in industry, and among the multitude of industries, focus on surface factors (manners, cursory behaviors, etc.), while appearing to address, through image-shaping campaigns, the deeper shared values of those cultures that constitute the environment. Yet, the deeper shared values at this level are of great concern, even of ultimate concern (Dalal, 2001; Newman, 1997). For example, what is the purpose of life? Why is there so much suffering? How can humans be so often cruel to one another?

At the environmental level, the world religions are a major force, providing meaning for billions of people throughout the world. These religions include Islam, Buddhism, Zen Buddhism, Christianity, Hinduism, and Judaism, and not just from an exoteric perspective, but also from a deeper esoteric—inner—perspective. It is very difficult for industries and businesses to address this level directly, because pleasing one faction often displeases another. Hence, most business/industry collectives are silent in this area. An alternative is to recognize common values in these various belief systems and incorporate these into a more inclusive general view (Chaudhuri, 1966; Smith, 2001; Spiegelberg, 1956).

Cultural philosophies underlie and help support each culture in originating life's meaning (Novak, 1994). Not only Western philosophers—Plato, Socrates, Spinoza, Kant, Hegel, etc.—but many others, such as Lao Tsu, Confucius, Pantanjahi, Gandhi, Aurobindo, Radha, Krishna, Siddhartha, Bodhi-dharma, Dogen, Rumi, and Muhammad, to list a few, have done this.

Political philosophy, too, has an immense influence at this level on understanding how the world is "as it is" (Toynbee, 1995). The range of political philosophy pans from democracy on one end of a continuum to totalitarian control on the other. Over the past fifteen years, democracy has been in favor throughout the world. While from a business perspective, this is positive, the by-product has all too often been a stark clash of various cultures, leading to conflict. This certainly was a factor leading to the tragedy on September 11, 2001 (Halliday, 2002). Stability of the environment requires that individuals see beyond cultural/political/religious differences, appreciating each system as *a* way, not as *the* way (Giddens, 1998; Smith, 1997). While this statement is highly idealistic, and most individuals will not achieve such an appreciation, it is critical that international business people do. That appreciation requires individuals to increase their cross-cultural knowledge, political knowledge, and religious understanding, and then integrate this knowledge into a more tolerant, inclusive viewpoint (Commons, et al., 1990; Sinnott, 1998; Karahan, 2000).

Throughout the environment are many variations on the themes of democracy and totalitarianism, involving various mixes of collectivism and individualism. For example, the writings of Karl Marx are very different than most business people imagine. They are not about enslaving the world by removing individualism. Instead, they provide a way to prevent dehumanizing workers (proletariat) by wealthy and all-powerful landowners (capitalists). I think it is safe to say that most of us who work have experienced the oppression of a selfish, egocentric business owner and have felt completely powerless. This is an unsatisfactory condition.

When opportunity for all is available, suspicion and deviousness can be sharply reduced. Remember the scathing attacks by Marx on capitalism. The shared values of the proletariat for opportunity and fairness were responsible for the Russian Revolution, which brought Lenin's version of communism to Russia. Recall also the civil wars in France, Spain, China, Vietnam, and in the South and Central Americas, the only option, finally, of the proletariat poor to gain rights and opportunity.

Notice, also, how governments that have avoided revolution in this century, such as Great Britain and the United States, have become more in tune with social-democratic belief systems, where the poor and down-trodden are not left to fend for themselves, but are aided by the government (Toynbee, 1995; Newman, 1997; Giddens, 1998). This is a clear incorporation of some socialist views into free enterprise systems, spurring self-motivation and, therefore, productivity.

None of us would like to be down-trodden without a way out. In this country, the government has "leveled the playing field," such that even the poorest U.S. citizens have access to quality education or training, if they are motivated (Garten, 2000). And, who does not want to reap increased profit if she or he chooses to work harder, a major benefit of a free capitalist enterprise? So a mixture of both the socialistic and capitalistic perspectives seems to be most valuable.

In our democratic way of being, we have seen the Democratic and Republican parties moving ever more toward each other to find a more balanced and tolerant political point of view that unites the most equitable of both liberal and conservative views.

The environment also contains and supports a broad variety of economic systems, including market economies, command economies, mixed economies, and state-directed economies (Samuelson & Nordhaus, 1985; Albaurn, et al., 1994). A pure market economy occurs when all economically productive activities are owned privately, rather than by the state. The goods and services a country produces, then, are the unique result of supply and demand interaction, not government intervention. This, of course, means that if demand is greater than supply, prices will rise and encourage increased production of that good or service. Conversely, if the supply of a product exceeds demand, prices will fall, and interest in producing more of that good or service will decline. In general, the purchasing trends of consumers—their wants and needs—determine both what is produced and in what quantity.

For a pure or free market to function, there can be no restrictions on supply, such as the monopolization of an industrial market by one firm (Samuelson & Nordhaus, 1985). If a monopoly exists, rather than increase output in response to greater demand, a monopolist may restrict production to force prices higher and reap increased profits. This situation is bad for the consumer, for the market, and for the country as a whole. Because a monopolist, by definition, has no competitors, there is no incentive for the monopolist to compete, and the market becomes ever more inefficient. Given the dangers of monopolies to a free-market economy, governments in free-market economies generally encourage vigorous, fair competition between private firms and outlaw monopolies. Private ownership assures that entrepreneurs and stockholders have a right to receive the profits generated by their efforts. This stimulates the entrepreneurs and stockholders to search for ever more efficient and innovative ways to serve the market (Jones & Neary, 1984).

In a command style of economy, the goods and services a country produces, the quantities produced, and the prices charged are planned and established by the state. This is consistent with the Marxist view that the government allocates resources for the "good of the society." In a true command economy, the government owns all the businesses and, ideally, can provide the goods and services that are of most benefit to the country as a whole.

Historically, a command economy has been a Marxist economy or, more specifically, a communist economy (Bartlett & Ghosshal, 1992; Albaurn, et al., 1994). But since the collapse of the Soviet Union, the number of command economies has dropped drastically. Although the idealized objective of the command economy is to mobilize economic resources for the common welfare, in practice, just the opposite is usually the result. In a state-owned system, there are few or no incentives to control costs, increase efficiency, or motivate workers, for one receives the same amount of money whether the job was high quality or average quality. Furthermore, because there is no competition, the state-controlled businesses cannot go out of business by being inefficient. And private ownership of business being absent, there is little individual incentive to serve consumers better.

In recent years, there has been a trend for market economies and command economies to become more united, incorporating the best of both systems. Many free-market economies have integrated some of the positive attributes of collectivist command economies (Giddens, 1998). That is, there are increased opportunities and benefits for all workers, such as education and/or training/retraining, minority preferences, unemployment insurance, disability compensation, and Social Security. This approach tends to retain the incentives of a capitalistic system, while providing the security of a collective system (Giddens, 1998). Also, a number of command economies have incorporated beneficial aspects of a market economy, such as limited private ownership. Today, it is difficult to speak of a pure market economy or a pure command economy, for most are mixed to some degree.

A mixed economy is a hybrid of the free-market and command economies. Certain sectors of business are owned privately, with the free-market approach left intact. Other sectors are state-owned, under the control of state planning. Mixed economies are very common in Western Europe—France, Italy, and Sweden being good examples. In a mixed economy, governments will intervene in business affairs when they believe it is in the best interests of the society to usurp private ownership. For example, Sweden has an extensive state-owned and directed health care system where there is universal "free" care for all citizens (Albaurn, et al., 1994).

A state-directed economy is one in which the government plays a key role in directing the investment activities of privately owned industries through "industrial policy." Industrial policy often takes the form of state subsidies to private enterprise in order to encourage them to increase activity in an industry deemed of strategic value to the country. For example, in Japan, the government subsidizes the vast majority of research and development required to support innovation in the semiconductor industry and enhance Japan's world lead (Hill, 2000). Most state-directed economies use the "infant" industry argument to justify their involvement in sheltering their industries from foreign competition. In order to protect their fledgling industries from large foreign economies of scale that have a huge competitive advantage, they erect trade barriers. These trade barriers are portrayed as protective devices necessary to overcoming their economic disadvantages.

The legal systems of countries that make up the environment establish rules, regulations, and laws to control business activity, both foreign and domestic, as well as define the grievance process (Toynbee, 1995; Karahan, 2000). The legal systems encountered in the environment (region-to-region, state-to-state, and country-to-country) are of immense importance to business, for they define the ways in which businesses can operate within the environment at large. Of particular interest to businesses—foreign and domestic—are contractual laws, monetary conversion procedures, property rights, patent rights, and trademark protection, as well as product safety requirements and liability laws.

Economics—macro and international—are very important to this level of operation (Samuelson & Nordhaus, 1985). Economic theory is rooted in the supply-and-demand cycle within each industry, as well as the cyclical economic structure of the entire environment (Besanko, et al., 2000). Economies are constantly interacting with other economies in terms of gross national product, balance of trade, labor costs, capital costs, and interest rates. Understanding the cyclical nature of economics, from both a country-to-country and a global perspective, is important. An industry, a country, or a region can have a major effect on the entire world economic situation. Basically, the goal of each nation, or union of nations, is to have a high economic output governed, to a large degree, by fiscal policy—taxation and spending policies. High levels of employment (low unemployment) can be influenced by governmental control of the money supply, which, in turn, affects interest rates. Price stability can be influenced directly by income policy (voluntary wage-price guidelines or mandatory controls). Foreign import-export balance is influenced by trade policy and exchange rate interventions.

Trade theory can be useful to an understanding of economics from a global perspective. In trade theory, the environment in which industries and companies do business is usually partitioned in terms of countries. Free trade, an important concept in trade theory, occurs when countries in the environment do not attempt to influence one another through trade quotas and restrictions as to what consumers of one can buy from another. Adam Smith argued that the free market, rather than government policy, should determine what countries in the environment import or export.

It has taken many decades for countries to fully realize the advantage of international trade as being in their best interest. In the past, the "mercantile" approach was used by many countries. This view posited that it was in the best interests of a country to maintain a trade surplus, that is, that exports should exceed imports. The flaw, however, is that such a policy creates winner and loser countries, a situation no longer feasible. Formerly, countries such as France and England colonized other countries to gain wealth at the expense of their colonies.

Years ago, Adam Smith attacked mercantilism, arguing that

countries differ in their abilities to produce goods (Bartlett & Ghosshal, 1992). He used as examples England, the most efficient textile manufacturer, and France, due to its more favorable climate, good soil, and expertise, the world's most efficient producer of wines. Hence, England had an "absolute" advantage in textile production and France in wine production. Smith went on to argue that countries should not try to meet all their needs internally, but should specialize in producing goods for which they had the absolute advantage.

David Ricardo, a nineteenth-century English economist, further expanded Smith's concept (Hill, 2000; Karahan, 2000). Ricardo argued that it made better sense for a country to specialize in producing those goods it is most efficient at producing and to buy goods it produces less efficiently. This would amount to income generated for all trade partners, because individual countries focus their resources on producing more of the products they produce most efficiently. This strategy is known generally as the "comparative advantage principle." Although it is an approach used in much of today's international business, it is vulnerable to one critical possibility—diminishing returns. That is, countries have an advantage employing this perspective, but only when there is unfailing demand for their good or service.

Swedish economists Eli Heckscher and Bertil Ohlin have taken a different perspective on this issue, a perspective often referred to as the Heckscher-Ohlin Theory. They argue that it is not greater productivity that provides a nation a comparative advantage, but rather, a nation's factor endowments, its resources (land, labor, and capital) (Bartlett & Ghosshal, 1992; Albaurn, et al., 1994; Karahan, 2000). Because different countries have different natural endowments, they also have different comparative advantages. This, of course, is advantageous to all. For example, the United States has long been a major exporter of grains due to its endowment of vast areas of farmable land. And it is interesting, as a sidenote, that agriculture, in the United States, is heavily government-subsidized. The Hecksher-Ohlin model has been used increasingly over the years, because of its simplicity (it has few assumptions) and its facility for no-nonsense prediction. Yet, as valuable as this model is, it is not without limitations. Wassily Leontief, the 1973 Nobel laureate in economics, pointed out that the United States' export products are not capital-intense, despite the United States having an abundant supply of capital, relative to other countries. This point, at variance with the Heckscher-Ohlin Theory, is known as "Leontief's Paradox." So, although the Heckscher-Ohlin Theory is not perfect, it remains a valuable tool for explaining important aspects of international trade.

In the mid-1960s, the economist Raymond Veron proposed what he termed the Product Life Cycle Theory of international trade dynamics (Hill, 2000; Montgomery & Porter, 1991). According to this theory, first-world, or advanced, nations develop and provide the bulk of innovative products and services to first-world consumers initially. But, over time, as competition increases and product/service differentiation becomes more difficult to achieve, those innovative products are then offered to less-developed nations, creating a whole new market. This perspective is generally true, but not absolute. First-world countries have not always been the first to develop new and innovative products/services.

In the 1970s, another perspective to understanding international trade emerged; it's referred to as the "New" Trade Theory. Its proponents argued that a country strong in producing and exporting a particular product is strong because it was likely the *first* country to offer it. The New Trade Theory, then, is simply the principle of the First Mover Advantage, understood at the industry level, applied to economies of large scale (Hill & Jones, 1999; Montgomery & Porter, 1991). And it is generally true that, for economies of large scale, the country that first introduces a product to the market will have a definite competitive advantage. But this is a tendency, not a law. There also exists a Late Mover Advantage that capitalizes on the mistakes of the First Mover, increasing product quality with much less front-end research and development cost (Porter, 1990; Karahan, 2000).

More recently, Harvard's Michael Porter and his team presented a new model, the National Competitive Advantage. From this model's perspective, a country's ability to compete successfully in exports depends upon four factors (Porter, 1980; 1990):

1. *Factor Endowments:* the country's production endowments, such as the skilled labor and the global infrastructure necessary to competing in the world marketplace. Note that these go beyond the basic endowment factors (land, labor, and capital) specified by Heckscher and Ohlin, to include "advanced" factors (research facilities, technological knowledge, communication infrastructure, etc.) that are found in technologically advanced nations.

2. *Demand Conditions:* the aggregate national demand for products and/or services. Markets where high quality is demanded nationally tend to make the industry more competitive globally.

3. *Related and Supporting Industries:* the presence or absence and strength or weakness of internal support industries that provide vital parts or raw materials for the production of national goods. If supporting industries are well furnished with particularly advanced factor endowments, these endowments tend to spill over into the main industry that exports products.

4. *Firm Strategy, Structure, and Rivalry:* "management ideologies" that either help or hinder national industries in building a competitive advantage. Additionally, vigorous national competition tends to create pressure to innovate,

improve products, and reduce costs, making the national industry more competitive in the world market.

None of the various theories we have reviewed can be considered the absolute truth, yet each contains a truth, that, when integrated with the others, creates a useful model with which to describe reality. Generally speaking, mercantilism is no longer a useful strategy. However, Smith's Absolute Economic Advantage perspective can be an effective strategy, particularly for post-industrial nations. And if demand were unlimited, the Comparative Advantage strategy would be more applicable than it is in actual practice. It is obvious that natural factor endowments (land, labor, location, and capital) are very important, but advanced factor endowments (communications infrastructure, managerial perspectives such as the integral business model, for example, sophisticated skills, technological know-how, research capability) are becoming more so, particularly as the move toward post-industrial societies continues. The First Mover principle we discussed in the New Trade Theory approach is very useful, but so is the Late Mover strategy. Finally, Porter's National Competitive Advantage Model is valuable and directly applicable to those industries that, because of national competition, are naturally "lean and mean" (and, therefore, "battle-hardened") and better able to compete in the international environment.

Subjective Quadrants

Unfortunately, each of the strategic perspectives reviewed above dismisses the entire subjective domain. If a nation, as a whole, is motivated to expand to the global environment, shared meaning will be critically important. Intersubjective values form the bedrock of social cultures, supplying the context for a society's norms (concepts of rights, political systems, truth, justice, honesty, loyalty, social obligations, collective responsibility, gender roles, love, relationships, sex, and marriage).

Cultures are greatly influenced by the prevailing political, economic, religious, philosophical, and legal structures of societies, and vice-versa. The basic component of any culture, however, is the individual and his or her own values, meaning, beliefs, aspirations, goals, and desires—all of which are shaped by culture. The individual and the collective are extensively interrelated, and this interrelationship has an enormous societal influence. For example, the degree of social stratification is influenced by whether the culture supports social mobility or a rigid caste system.

In the late 1960s, Goert Hofstede, a psychologist employed by IBM, proposed a model to predict how cultural differences translate to values and meaning in the workplace (Hill, 2000; Karahan, 2000). He identified four key variables he claimed would allow this prediction: 1) power distance, 2) avoidance of uncertainty, 3) individualism versus collectivism, and 4) gender issues, or masculinity versus femininity. The power distance dimension refers to the manner in which a particular culture deals with individuals differing in wealth and power. He found when power distances in a culture were high, a high degree of disparity existed between those with wealth and power and those without, and when the power distances were low, there was minor disparity. In fact, cultures having low power distances tended to negate inequalities through active education policies.

Uncertainty avoidance measures the extent to which cultures differ, on the average, in dealing with ambiguity and uncertainty. Members belonging to high uncertainty avoidance cultures place much value on job security, career stability, and retirement benefits, as well as much structure in the job. Low uncertainty avoidance cultures are more ready to take risks to attain their goals, look for job satisfaction over security, and resent all but minimum job structuring.

The individualism-versus-collectivism component is used to

measure the relationship between the employee and his or her fellow workers. In cultures that promote individualism, ties between employees are loose, but individual achievement and freedom are highly valued. In cultures that emphasize group collective values, workers tend to form extended families and relationships on the job to look after one another, not as individuals, but as team members.

The gender—masculinity versus femininity—dimension measures whether the culture is a traditionally masculine one or a feminine one (Hofstede's term). In a feminine culture, gender roles tend not to be specifically defined and differentiated, as they are in a masculine one.

Within the competitive environment, most industries form alliances to assure uniform quality, as well as to develop the industry more fully. For example, ASTM (American Society for Testing and Materials) is a multi-industrial group that meets every six months to discuss ways to assure quality through uniform testing and evaluation methods. Others, such as the American Medical Association, American Bar Association, and the Newspaper Guild, have similar interests in improving quality and controlling lack thereof. Such groups, although obviously interested in promoting their industry, also want to establish self-control of quality to avoid, for example, outside governmental controls and regulations. In cases where governmental controls exist (for example, the FDA for the drug industry), affected industries tend to work with and, if possible, influence government policy as a unified industry group. At these inter-firm meetings, general self-control procedures are established, which serve as rules and regulations to promote quality products and services, fair prices, and adequately trained, qualified technical people. Some groups require proficiency tests (board certifications) for personnel to assure further a standardized high quality of service.

These types of industrial organizations also provide a way individuals can intersubjectively bond with other professionals sharing similar, broad-view interests. Such interaction facilitates emotional bonding, and it also serves as a voluntary means for sharing information—a cross-pollination process—so a company does not get "in-bred."

Summary

As we have seen, Hofstede provided valuable insights into how individuals from different cultures relate in the workplace. This is important information, particularly in managing companies across borders. Recall that, within the environment, behavior of groups is, in part, influenced and determined by social, political, economic, and legal conditions. Hence, sociological theory, political theory, world demographics (first-world, second-world, and third-world countries), economic theory (Adam Smith's free-market economy to Karl Marx's collectivism), legal systems, and international trade theory—Adam Smith's Absolute Advantage; David Ricardo's Comparative Advantage; Heckscher-Ohlin's Theory of Factor Endowments (land, labor, capital), tempered by the Leontief Paradox; Raymond Veron's Product Life Cycle theory; the New Trade theory and its First Mover Advantage postulate; and Michael Porter's National Competitive Advantage theory—are all important influences on the business world. Moreover, they are important in integral business, for they provide general business conditions that must be understood and applied in order to flourish in the coming years.

A summary chart of the environmental level is provided in Figure 6-1.

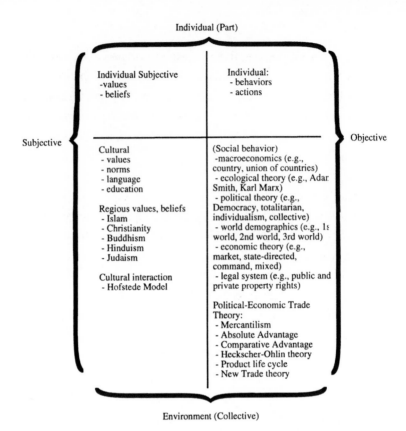

Figure 6-1. Individual-Environmental Level Quadrant Model

Integration: Integral Business Paradigm

The overriding focus of the Integral Business Paradigm is to link the four levels of business hierarchy (each level consisting of the four quadrants) into a seamless whole. The levels, like the quadrants, are distinct but not separate from one another. This allows one to perceive more accurately and comprehensively the total business environment as it is and, thus, to *compete in* and *contribute to* oneself, one's team, one's company, the industry, and the environment—the world village—more effectively. In my view, business, like so many human institutions, has erred in over-specializing within specific business disciplines (e.g., finance, accounting, operations, sales and marketing, etc.). This action ignores the breadth of a full-quadrant perspective (subjective, intersubjective, and objective) and the depth of the employee, team, company, industry, and environment continuum, so that one never comprehends the entire picture, from entry-level employees all the way to the CEO and board of directors. This has engendered a selective, short-run focus. However useful a short-run focus is, and it has its place, a long-term focus is also necessary.

Figure 6-2 presents the complete Integral Business Model, in which the individual is in constant interaction with the objective and subjective aspects of the team, the company, the firm, the industry, and the environment, whether acknowledged or not.

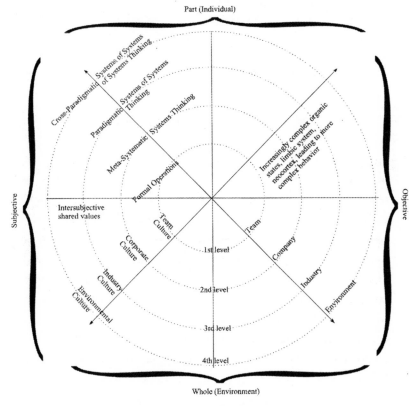

Figure 6-2. Integral Business Model

Within the environment is situated the collection of industries and within each industry, firms are situated. Most business strategy is based on company reaction relative to the industry. Although this is an important view, it is incomplete. Equally important to businesses are the teams (sections, departments, divisions) upon which it is functionally dependent, as well as the contribution of each employee, the most fundamental component of the entire schema. The integral business perspective offers a sliding continuum, extending from the relationship a person has to the team through the relationship to the environment, while encompassing the companies and industries that connect them (see Figure 6-3).

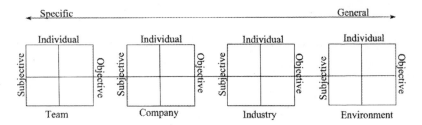

Figure 6-3. Integral Business Continuum

As stated so many times, each of the four vertical levels is composed of the four quadrants, each of the four having equal importance. To become more competitive, yet more compassionate and caring, will require incorporating the different levels with knowledge of the subjective, intersubjective, and objective domains at each. Fortunately, the information applicable to each dimension and hierarchical level is readily available now. All one has to do is acquire it, apply it, and develop it in one's own vision.

Beyond a competitive advantage, the integral business model can help one bring together, through synthesis, the information gathered by analysis and to see its relevance not only to profit, but to enhancement of the quality of human lives throughout the world.

Indeed, it is our responsibility to husband this information to enhance life, not simply provide more for those who already have too much unearned wealth, too much unbridled power, and too much self-importance. By incorporating subjective and intersubjective domains, we have a way of redefining character, because value, not just fact, is important. Integral business is about care, concern, wisdom, fairness, character, truthfulness—and making a profit. But, it does not sell out to profit only, a position no longer acceptable in today's world. Business now must not only take profits, but reinvest them to the betterment of all who occupy the globe. Business, like other human endeavors, must no longer look the other way to avoid acknowledging the suffering of others around this planet (Drucker, 1993; 1995).

In conclusion, the concept of integral business is merely an integration of the best visions and practices of business, psychology, sociology, cultural studies, politics, systems-thinking, economics, and human science, and the synthesis of this knowledge into a growth bloom of possibilities for all humanity in the twenty-first century.

CHAPTER 7

Transformation Through the Courage to Contribute

We have discussed, over the preceding chapters, the integral business perspective, which can foster more effective business practices that not only add to the bottom line, but to the social welfare through personal compassion and care in business transactions. This is a business responsibility, because business controls the global power.

The focus of the concept is on acquiring knowledge and applying that knowledge both vertically and horizontally, in order to contribute not only to oneself, one's meaning, one's family, or one's group, but to all humanity. This endeavor will be difficult to pursue, but it can provide meaning that transcends the apparent absurdity of life. The price to pay for successful contribution will be the courage to stand up for one's principles. It is not enough to have knowledge and wisdom about what is right; one must also act. All too often, positive action is halted by fear of being singled out, hurt, rejected, fired, or even killed. That did not stop ordinary people from preventing a fourth jet airplane crash on September 11, 2001, on the White House or the United States Capitol building. Todd Beamer, Mark Bingham, Tom Burnett, Jeremy Glick, and Lou Nacke, passengers on American Airlines Flight 93, rose to the occasion to avoid being victims, and to exercise their personal options to say "no," resoundingly. It cost them their lives. Courage is the ability to attend to a task, in spite of gut-wrenching fear.

One of the first steps to attaining courage to act is to acknowledge, from an existential position, that one is essentially "alone," alone with one's self and one's experience. No one else sees things exactly like you, no one feels exactly like you, and no one can know you exactly as you know yourself. But out of this aloneness, you can discover a deeper, more real Self, a discovery that ultimately provides both unrivaled courage and satisfaction (Assagioli, 1965).

Discovery of one's real Self takes time; it is rarely an immediate discovery. Contribution to fair business practices, in spite of one's doubts and fears of being vulnerable, requires not only a high level of courage, but persistent courage (Paulson, 1999). This is often a time of great personal upheaval, for one realizes that she or he cannot go back to the "old" ways of conducting business, yet does not feel comfortable with the "new" ways. This is a time when one must reach deep within for the will to continue, despite the feeling of existing in limbo.

As individuals in business begin to accept who they are authentically, and truly strive to become that person, they often will find that they no longer "fit in" with their business peers. The business tasks they used to do, the money and perks they collected, as well as the business people they once admired, are of diminished personal value. This is a lonely time, requiring courage "to begin anew" and to live in accordance with newfound inner truth. At times when danger threatens to paralyze, suddenly, from the depths of our being, surges an unsuspected strength "enabling us to place a firm foot on the edge of the precipice" and confront an unfairness calmly and resolutely, standing by our convictions at all costs.

I am reminded of Dietrich Bonhoeffer, a German Lutheran theologian, who was safely out of Germany and Hitler's Nazi reign of terror in the late 1930s (Bonhoeffer, 1949). He, a business man in the religious field, resisted the oppression and systematic extermination of the Jews, Gypsies, communists, and other "inferior" peoples. He would not ignore or explain away this inhumane action.

He committed himself to living truth as he saw it, which meant he had to stand up for what he believed and contribute to human fairness and dignity. Consequently, he was fired, "shot dead," in 1943, which, for him, was the cost of being true to his values. He understood courage to be living authentically in this life "now," by contributing to humanity openly, justly, and with dignity, not awaiting his reward upon "retirement" in a heavenly afterlife.

Courage to be oneself authentically comes at a price; it is not free of negative repercussions. To walk away from a toxic job, or to take a stand against unfairness, may be met with the loss of a profession, of profit, or, in the extreme, of one's life. But what do you have if you have no values and no respect?

Courage to be yourself, then, is not only the discovery of who you are authentically but also demands that you live in a way consistent with that self-discovery. That is, you make your own choices, listen to your own voice for guidance, and act based upon your own tastes and preferences, while taking into account the impact of your actions upon others in keeping with what is just and fair. Courage to be yourself requires a committed, conscious relationship with yourself, deepening to the very source of your Being. It requires seeking your deepest inner truth, no matter where the journey may lead.

That is not to say wrongdoing is overlooked, let alone condoned or accepted. No, courage is not blind. It works hand in hand with morality. If any condemnation or punishment is warranted, it arises from moral indignation, but that indignation is directed at behavior, not beingness: "Hate the sin but love the sinner." The courage to be is personally caring, unconditionally so, and universally compassionate, even as corrective action is taken or punishment administered.

Finding the courage to be oneself enables one to accept others for failing to understand, or even respect, other human beings. It even allows one to forgive all humanity for its senseless cruelties imposed upon the poor, the weak, or those who do not fit in. The courage to be oneself fosters the self-empowerment necessary to granting that forgiveness.

In the future, I believe we must find the courage not only to come together in teams, in companies, in industries, and in countries, through action, but also as humans seeking mutual understanding and acceptance. Such courage requires that each of us step out of the safety of our familiar dogmas, policies, and group biases, to decide authentically what is true, what is right, and what is just, and to act accordingly. Most of us have searched for the courage "to do the right thing" in business groups, in temples, in churches, in science, in medicine, on earth, in heaven, and even in hell. But, in the end, sometimes in despair, we come back to ourselves—where the whole search began—and find that what each of us has been seeking without abides within. It is our own authentic Self—our source of Being—with us all the time and awaiting discovery. And from this position, we *will* act with care and compassion.

Notes

[1] Epistemology, the study of how one knows something to be true, is usually applied to assure the data collection/processing and its meaning are valid. In my research, much of what business strategists—not all, however—do with provided data is to crank it through a quantitative analysis computer subroutine to "generate the numbers." It may be via forecasting, use of Bayesian decision models (particularly in assigning event probabilities), simulation modeling, game theory, branch and bound methods computing integer linear programming models, inventory control models, project management (e.g., PERT, CPM), or linear programming, using graphical analysis or a Simplex algorithm. Whatever, a validation of these methods (restrictions, assumptions, and confidence levels for Type I and II errors) should be completed.

Generally, the strategist:
  defines the problem
  develops a model
  acquires input data for model
  acquires solution (strategy)
  tests solutions
  analyzes the sensitivity/specificity/reliability
  implements strategy.

At each of these points, errors, omissions, and assumptions may creep in. And perhaps the greatest error is the belief that data are measured without error. Finally, the greatest benefit of an analysis often is the "subjective" sense of *situational control* it provides management, like a lucky rabbit's foot.

2 In the human sciences, which deal with human social constructions of reality, both first-person (personal subjective) and second-person (intersubjective) perspectives are deemed critical to better understanding a human-created system—business, in this case. Additionally, in human science as well as in empirical science, third-person views (objective domain) are equally important. Unfortunately, empirical science recognizes this view as the only "real" view, and being blind to first- and second-person perspectives weakens the ability to discover biases inherent to concept usage, interpretations, and in psychological defense mechanisms. This often is not a practical problem in empirical science when measuring phenomena such as weight, velocity, volume, mass, height, etc. But it can be very problematic in evaluating human social reality—business operations, and so on—and trying to decide what course of action to take. This, in no way, argues for the preference of first-, second-, or third-person (subjective, intersubjective, objective) domains, only that they each be recognized. The human sciences have, for years, bickered as to whether empirical science procedures can be used, or whether the human sciences should develop their own. My view is that both should be used, as appropriate.

3 The acronym SWOT stands for Strength and Weakness (of company) and Opportunities and Threats (of industry). A strength is a company's proficiency or a characteristic that provides enhanced competitiveness. Examples include special skills/expertise, valuable physical assets, valuable human assets, valuable organizational assets, valuable intangible assets, company capabilities, market position, and strategic alliances. Weaknesses are things a firm is not proficient in or lacks, putting it at a disadvantage. Disadvantages include deficiencies in competitively important skills or knowledge, lack of competitively important physical, human, organizational, or intangible assets and/or lack of com-

petitive capabilities in key areas. Industry opportunity is a huge factor in shaping a company's strategy: opportunities include high demand for company products/services and favorable industry conditions. The opportunities must offer important growth potential that is profitable, where a company has a competitive advantage, and match well with the financial/organizational capabilities of the firm. Industry threats include the emergence of cheaper technologies, rivals introducing better products/services, entry of low-cost foreign competitors, and new governmental regulations more burdensome to the company than to other competitors, and so on.

References

Agor, W. H. (1984). *Intuitive management: Integrating left and right brain management skills.* Englewood Cliffs, NJ: Prentice-Hall.

Agor, W. H. (1986). *The logic of intuitive decision making.* Westport, CT: Greenwood Press.

Albaurn, G., Stranskov, J., Duer, E., & Dowd, L. (1994). *International marketing and export management.* 2nd ed. Workingham, UK: Addison-Wesley.

Alexander, J. C. (1982). *Theoretical logic in sociology,* vol. 1. Berkeley: University of California.

Anderson, R. A. (1987). *Wellness medicine.* Lynnwood, WA: American Health Press.

Anderson, W. T. (1995). *The truth about the truth.* New York: Tarcher.

Angyal, A. (1965). *Neurosis and treatment: A holistic theory.* New York: John Wiley & Sons.

Argyris, C. (1964). *Integrating the individual and the organization.* New York: John Wiley.

Argyris, C . (1982). *Reasoning, learning and action.* San Francisco: Jossey-Bass.

Argyris, C. (1992). *On organizational learning.* Cambridge, MA: Blackwell.

Argyris, C. (1993). *Knowledge for action.* San Francisco: Jossey-Bass.

Assagioli, R. (1965). *Psychosynthesis.* New York: Hobbs, Dorman & Company.

Banathy, B. (1996). *Designing social systems in a changing world.* New York: Plenon Press.

Bandura, A. (1997). *Self efficacy.* New York: Freeman.

Barasch, M. I. (2000). *Healing dreams.* New York: Riverhead Books.

Barnard, C. I. (1968). *Functions of the executive,* 30th anniversary ed. Cambridge, MA: Harvard University Press.

Bartlett, C. A. & Ghosshal, S. (1992). *Transnational management.* Boston: Irwin.

Bennis, W. & Nanus, B. (1985). *Leaders: The strategies for taking charge.* New York: Harper & Row.

Bertalanffy, L. Von. (1968). *General system theory.* New York: Braziller.

Besanko, D., Dranove, D., & Shanley, M. (2000). *Economics of strategy,* 2nd ed. New York: Wiley.

Bonhoeffer, D. (1949). *The cost of discipleship*. Rev. ed. New York: MacMillan Co.

Borg, W. R. & Gall, M. D. (1989). *Educational research*, 5th ed. New York: Longman.

Bowerman, B. L. & O'Connell, R. T. (1979). *Time series and forecasting*. Belmont, CA: Duxburg Press.

Bringham, E. F., Grapenski, L. C., & Ehrhardt, M. C. (1999). *Financial management: Theory and practice*, 9th ed. Orlando, FL: Harcourt College Publishers.

Brooks, E. & Odiorne, G. S. (1984). *Managing by negotiation*. New York: Van Nostrand Reinhold.

Brown, L. R. (1997). *State of the world*. New York: Norton.

Bugental, J. F. T. (1965). *The search for authenticity*. New York: Holt, Rinehart and Winston.

Cahoone, L. E. (1996). *From modernism to postmodernism*. Cambridge, MA: Blackwell.

Chaudhuri, H. (1966). *Modern man's religion*. Santa Barbara: Rowny Press.

Collins, E. G. C. (1983). *Executive success: Making it in management*. New York: John Wiley & Sons.

Commons, M. L., Armon, C., Kohlberg, L., Richards, F. A., Gretzner, T. A., & Sinnott, J. D. (1990). *Adult development,* vol. 1 and 2. New York: Praeger.

Cooper, R. K. (1989). *Health and fitness excellence.* Boston: Houghton-Mifflin.

Copleston, F. (1993). *A history of philosophy: Greece and Rome,* vol. 1. New York: Doubleday.

Crawford, A. (2002). Personal communication. University of Montana, School of Business Administration, Missoula, MT.

Creech, B. (1994). *The five pillars of TQM.* New York: Dutton.

Culp, G. & Smith, A. (1992). *Managing people for project success.* New York: John Wiley & Sons.

Dalal, A. S. (2001). *A greater psychology: An introduction into the psychological thought of Sri Aurobindo.* New York: Tarcher.

Davidson, D. (2001). *Subjective, intersubjective, objective.* New York: Oxford University Press.

Deal, T. E. & Kennedy, A. A. (1982). *Corporate cultures.* Reading, MA: Addison-Wesley.

Deming, W. E. (1982). *Out of crisis.* Cambridge, MA: Massachusetts Institute of Technology.

Deutsch, E. (2001). *Persons and valuable worlds: A global philosophy.* New York: Rowman & Littlefield.

Dilworth, J. B. (1979). *Production and operations management.* New York: Random House.

Drucker, P. F. (1964). *Managing for results.* New York: Harper & Row.

Drucker, P. F. (1967). *The effective executive.* New York: Harper & Row.

Drucker, P. F. (1974). *Management: Tasks, responsibilities, practices.* New York: Harper & Row.

Drucker, P. F. (1985). *The innovator and entrepreneur.* New York: Harper & Row.

Drucker, P. F. (1993). *Post-capitalistic society.* New York: Harper-Collins.

Drucker, P. F. (1995). *Managing in a time of great change.* New York: Penguin.

Dyson, F. (1979). *Disturbing the universe.* New York: Harper & Row.

Edlin, G., Golanty, E., & McCormack-Brown, K. (1996). *Health and wellness*, 5th ed. Sudbury, MA: Jones & Bartlett.

Egan, G. (1998). *The skilled helper: A problem-management approach to helping*, 6th ed. Pacific Grove, CA: Brooks/Cole Publishing.

Evans, J. R. & Lindsay, W. M. (1999). *The management and control of quality*, 4th ed. Cincinnati: Southwestern College.

Fadiman, J. & Frager, R. (2002). *Personality and personal growth*, 5th ed. Upper Saddle River, NJ: Prentice-Hall.

Fahey, L. & Randall, R. M. (1998). *Learning from the future: Competitive foresight scenarios*. New York: John Wiley & Sons.

Frankl, V. E. (1959). *Man's search for meaning*. Boston: Beacon Press.

Frankl, V. E. (1969). *The will to meaning*. New York: New American Library.

Fromm, E. (1968). *The revolution of hope*. New York: Harper & Row.

Gardner, H., Csikszentmihalyi, M., & Damon, W. (2001). *Good work: When excellence and ethics meet*. New York: Basic Books.

Garten, J. E. (2000). *World view*. Boston: Harvard Business Press.

Geertz, C. (1973). *The interpretation of cultures*. New York: Basic Books.

Gerard, R. (1995). Personal discussion with Robert Gerard, Ph.D., Director, International Foundation for Integral Psychology. 1092 Wilshire Boulevard, Los Angeles, CA 90024.

Gharajedaghi, J. (1999). *Systems thinking: Managing chaos and complexity*. Boston: Butterworth-Hein-Mann.

Gibson, J. L., Ivancevich, J. M & Donnelly, J. H. (1979). *Organizations: Behavior, structure, process*. 3rd ed. Dallas, TX: Irwin-Dossey.

Giddens, A. (1998). *The third way*. Madeline, MA: Blackwell.

Gilligan, C. (1982). *In a different voice: Psychological theory of women's development*. Cambridge, MA: Harvard University Press.

Grimblatt, M. & Titan, S. (2002). *Financial markets and corporate strategy*, 2nd ed. New York: McGraw-Hill-Irwin.

Halliday, F. (2002). *Two hours that shook the world: September 11, 2001 causes and consequences*. London: Saqi Books.

Hamel, G. & Prahalad, C. K. (1994). *Competing for the future*. Cambridge, MD: Harvard Business School Press.

Hampden-Turner, G. (1990). *Creating corporate culture*. Reading, MA: Addison-Wesley.

Handy, C. (1998). *The hungry spirit*. New York: Broadway Books.

Harvey, D. (1990). *The condition of post modernity*. Cambridge: Blackwell Publishers.

Hersey, P. & Blanchard, K. H. (1993). *Management of organizational behavior*, 6th ed. Englewood Cliffs, NJ: Prentice-Hall.

Hershey, P., Blanchard, K. H., & Johnson, D. E. (1996). *Management of organizational behavior,* 7th ed. Upper Saddle River, NJ: Prentice-Hall.

Higgins, R. C. (2001). *Analysis for financial management*, 6th ed. New York: McGraw-Hill.

Hill, C. W. L. (2000). *International business*, 3rd ed. New York: McGraw-Hill.

Hill, C. W. L & Jones, C. R. (1998). *Strategic Management,* 4th ed. Boston: Houghton-Mifflin.

Hillier, F. S. & Lieberman, G. J. (1980). *Introduction to operations research*, 3rd ed. San Francisco: Holden-Day.

Hitt, M. A., Ireland, R. D., & Hoskissoh, R. E. (1999). *Strategic Management,* 3rd ed. New York: South Western College Publishing.

Horngren, C. T. (1984). *Introduction to management accounting*, 5th ed. Englewood Cliffs, NJ: Prentice-Hall.

Horngren, C. T., Sundem, G. L. & Statton, W. O. (1999). *Introduction to management accounting*, 11th ed. Upper Saddle River, NJ: Prentice-Hall.

Hunter, J. D. (2000). *The death of character: Moral education in an age without good or evil.* New York: Basic Books.

Illich, J. (1973). *The art and skill of successful negotiations.* Englewood Cliffs, NJ: Prentice-Hall.

Jackendorf, R. (2002). *Foundations of language.* New York: Oxford University Press.

Jones R. W. & Neary, J. P. (1984). "The positive theory of international trade." Jones, R. W. & Kenen, P. B. Eds. *Handbook of international economics.* Amesterdam: North Holland Press.

Jung, C. G. (1969). The archetypes and the collective unconscious, 2nd ed., vol. 9.1, *Collected Works.* Princeton: Princeton University Press.

Kaku, M. (1997). *Visions: How science will revolutionize the 21st century.* New York: Anchor Books.

Kanter, R. A. (1983). *The change masters.* New York: Simon & Schuster.

Kao, J. J. (1989). *Entrepreneurship, creativity, and organization.* Englewood Cliffs, NJ: Prentice-Hall.

Karahan, R. S. (2000). *Globalization of business.* Personal Communication. Bozeman, MT: Montana State University.

Kegan, R. (1994). *In over our heads.* Cambridge, MA: Harvard University Press.

Kekes, J. (1995). *Moral wisdom and the good life*. Ithaca, NY: Cornell University Press.

Kelley, R. E. (1985). *The gold collar worker*. Reading, MA: Addison-Wesley.

Kelly, G. (1955). *The psychology of personal constructs* (two volumes). New York: Norton.

Koestler, A. (1976). *The ghost in the machine*. New York: Random House.

Kolb, D. A., Rubin, I. M., & Mcintyre, J. M. (1983). *Organizational psychology*, 4th ed. Englewood Cliffs, NJ: Prentice-Hall.

Kuhn, T. (1970). *The structure of scientific revolutions*. Chicago: University of Chicago Press.

Lapin, L. L. (1991). *Quantitative methods for business decisions*. New York: Harcourt Brace Jovanovich.

Lowendahl, B. R. (1997). *Strategic management of professional service firms*. Copenhagen: Handelshojskolens Forlag.

Makridakis, S. G. & Wheelwright, S. C. (1978). *Forecasting*. New York: John Wiley.

Maslow, A. H. (1971). *The farther reaches of human nature*. New York: Viking Press.

Maslow, A. H. (1954). *Motivation and personality*. New York: Harper & Row.

May, R. (1953). *Man's search for himself*. New York: Norton.

May, R. (1977). *The meaning of anxiety*. New York: Norton.

McCarthy, T. (1978). *The critical theory of Jürgen Habermas*. Cambridge, MA: MIT Press.

Merton, R. K. (1957). *Social theory and social structure*. Glencoe, IL: Free Press.

Mintzberg, H. & Quinn, J. B. (1996). *The strategy process*. 3rd ed. Upper Saddle River, NJ: Prentice-Hall.

Mintzberg, H., Ahlstrand, B., & Lampel, J. (1998). *Strategic safari*. New York: Free Press.

Monte, C. F. (1971). *Beneath the mask*. New York: Praeger Publishing.

Monte, C. F. (1999). *Beneath the mask,* 6th ed. New York: Harcourt Brace.

Montgomery, C. A. & Porter, M. E. (1991). *Harvard business review: Strategy*. Boston: Harvard Business Press.

Moore, T. (1992). *Care of the soul*. New York: HarperCollins.

Murti, T. R. V. (1955). *The central philosophy of Buddhism: A study of the Mâdhyamika system*. New Delhi: Munshiran Manoharlal.

Newman, D. M. (1997). *Sociology*. Thousand Oaks, CA: Sage.

Neter, J. & Wasserman, W. (1974). *Applied linear statistical models*. Homewood, IL: Richard D. Irwin.

Novak, P. (1994). *The world's wisdom*. New York: Harper & Row.

Odiorne, G. S. (1969). *Management decisions by objectives*. Englewood Cliffs, NJ: Prentice-Hall.

Oster, S. M. (1999). *Modern competitive analysis*, 3rd ed. New York: Oxford University Press.

Osterberg, R. (1993). *Corporate renaissance*. Mill Valley, CA: Nataraj.

Ousbourne, J. (2002). "How to work a room." *MBA Jungle.* New York: Jungle Media Group, Mar/Apr, pp. 44–45.

Paulson, D. S. (1994). *Walking the point: Male initiation and the Vietnam experience*. Plantation, FL: Distinctive Press.

Paulson, D. S. (1997, December). "Developing effective topical antimicrobials." *Soaps/Cosmetics/Chemical Specialties*, pp. 37–42

Paulson, D. S. (1999, Fall). "Courage to be oneself." *Voices: Journal of the American Academy of Psychotherapists*, pp. 56–58.

Paulson, D. S. (2001, December). "New ideas for successful product development." *Soaps/Cosmetics/Chemical Specialties*, pp. 72–79.

Paulson, D. S. & Vogel, D. G. (1984, May). "Preparatory software documentation for validation of computer controlled manufacturing operations." *Pharmaceutical manufacturing*, pp. 21–30.

Paulson, D. S. & Van Woert, R. (1984, October). "Inventory models for controlling solid dosage production cycles." *Pharmaceutical engineering*, pp. 56–59.

Paulson, D. S. & Van Woert, R. (1985, May/June). "A method of determining optimum product mix." *Pharmaceutical engineering*, pp. 14–20.

Peters, T. (1987). *Thriving on chaos*. New York: Alfred A. Knopf.

Polkinghorne, D. (1983). *Methodology for the human sciences*. Albany, NY: SUNY.

Porter, M. (1980). *Competitive strategy*. New York: Free Press.

Porter, M. (1985). *Competitive advantage*. New York: Free Press.

Porter, M. (1990). *The competitive advantage of nations*. New York: Free Press.

Post, S. G. (2002). "Introduction," *Altruism and altruistic love: Science, philosophy, and religion in dialogue*. Post, S. G., Underwood, L. G., Schloss, J. P., & Hurlburt, W. B., eds. New York: Oxford University Press.

Ramanan, K. V. (1975). *Nargarjuna's philosophy*. Delhi: Motilal Banarsidass.

Remen, N. (1980). *The human patient*. Garden City, NY: Anchor.

Render, B. & Stair, R. M. (2000). *Quantitative analysis for management*, 7th ed. Upper Saddle River, NJ: Prentice-Hall.

Saussure, F. (1959). *Course in general linguistics*. New York: Philosophical Library.

Samuelson, P. A. & Nordhaus, W. D. (1995). *Economics*, 15th ed. New York: McGraw-Hill.

Schneider, K. J. & May, R. (1995). *The psychology of existence*. New York: McGraw-Hill.

Searle, J. R. (1995). *The construction of social reality*. New York: Free Press.

Senge, P. M. (1990). *The fifth discipline*. New York: Doubleday-Currency.

Sinnott, J. D. (1994). *Interdisciplinary handbook of adult lifespan learning*. Westport, CT: Greenwood Press.

Sinnott, J. D. (1998). *The development of logic in adulthood*. New York: Plenum.

Smart, N. (1999). *World philosophies*. New York: Routledge.

Smith, H. (2001). *Why religion matters*. San Francisco: Harper.

Smith, R. (1997). *The Norton history of the human sciences*. New York: W. W. Norton.

Sorokin, P. A. (1954). *The ways and power of love*. Boston: Beacon Press.

Spiegelberg, F. (1956). *Living religions of the world*. Englewood Cliffs, NJ: Prentice-Hall.

Sterman, J. D. (2000). *Business dynamics: Systems thinking and modeling for a complex world*. New York: McGraw-Hill.

Stoner, J. A. F. (1982). *Management*, 2nd ed. Englewood Cliffs, NJ: Prentice-Hall.

Teyber, E. (2000). *Interpersonal process of psychotherapy*, 4th ed. Belmont, CA: Wadsworth.

Toynbee, A. (1995). *A study of history*. New York: Barnes & Noble.

Vaughan, F. (1995). *The inward arc*, 2nd ed. Grass Valley, CA: Blue Dolphin.

Wall, B., Solum, R. S., & Sobel, M. R. (1992). *The visionary leader.* Rocklin, CA: Prima Publishing.

Walsh, R. (1984). *Staying alive.* Boston: New Science Library.

Walsh, R. & Shapiro, D. H. (1983). *Beyond health and normality.* New York: Van Nostrand, Reinhold.

Walsh, R & Vaughan, F. (1993). *Paths beyond ego: The transpersonal vision.* Los Angeles: Tarcher.

Wilber, K. (1995). *Sex, ecology, spirituality: The spirituality of evolution.* Boston: Shambhala.

Wilber, K. (1996). *A brief history of everything.* Boston: Shambhala.

Wilber, K. (1997). *The eye of the spirit.* Boston: Shambhala.

Wilber, K. (1998). *The marriage of sense and soul: Integrating science and religion.* New York: Random House.

Wilber, K. (2000a). *The collected works,* vol. 6. Boston: Shambhala.

Wilber, K. (2000b). *A theory of everything.* Boston: Shambhala.

Wilber, K. (2002). *Boomeritis: A novel that will set you free.* Boston: Shambhala.

Wurthnow, R. (1995). *Learning to care.* New York: Oxford University Press.

Acknowledgments

In writing this book, I have been influenced by many disciplines, not just business. Years ago, after finishing graduate school as a student in microbiology and biostatistics. I would have been killed by the business system, for which academia had so poorly trained me, had it not been for Rod A. Marshall, then the Executive Vice President of Skyland Scientific Services. Rod took me as a "beat up" and "defeated" technical person and exposed me to the business world in terms of self-discipline, service, concern for others, compromise, and entrepreneurship. While far from a finished product, that mentoring ultimately enabled me to launch my own biotechnology firm grounded in science, business, and psychology in 1991.

I wrote this book in part based on my own frustration with the current business system, culminating in the Enron, WorldCom, and Qwest deceptions in their accounting practices. Clearly, the situation is not only the fault of current CEOs or financial auditors, but of the entire business system, fueled by pressures of higher returns for investors, who, themselves, are becoming increasingly vulnerable.

Based on my research, I cannot find anyone who is comfortable with the system as it is. CEOs and upper management feel they function only to provide the mission demanded by the Board of Directors. They clearly know the Board and the investors hold no loyalty to them. They cannot grow personally or professionally at reasonable, disciplined rates or become more humanistic in their treatment of employees. This requires more time than investors will commit, and they will simply invest in firms that will generate an increased value to them. Investors, in turn, are pressured by their situations. They do not intend for the system to be as it is, but it *is* the way it is. Employees learn quickly that survival often is not only working hard, but working ruthless. The federal government is also in a quandary, for a society at war with itself is in jeopardy of collapse.

Nowhere is this situation desired by anyone. It has taken on a life of its own, forcing each of us to work every harder just to keep what we have. This book is not about turning our backs on capitalism, our culture, or the system. It is about designing and implementing a system that is fair to those who contribute, planning with foresight to meet human long-term needs, and approaching business with a practicality that can be applied today. This endeavor will require that we see the system in its entirety, not just the common, isolated components, which are caught up in the system's ever increasing complexity. In this book, we shall construct a way out that iwll be suitable for all parties, given realism, restraint, and discipline are applied.

Others who have inspired me, some of whom I personally know, and others whom I do not, include: Robert Assagioli, MD, Robert Gerard, Ph.D., Peter Drucker, Carl G. Jung, Abraham Maslow, Robert Kegan, Ph.D., Edith Stauffer, Ph.D., Louis Pasteur, Earl Nightingale, Frances Vaughan, Ph.D., Roger Walsh, MD, and Edward Shubat, Ph.D.

I also thank John Mitchell, Ph.D., for his valuable assistance in editing this book, and Tammy Anderson, for superbly managing the entire process. Thanks to John White for pounding the pavement to sell this book to a publisher, and to Patrick Huyghe and Paraview Press for their help, professional editing, smoothing, and direction.

ABOUT THE AUTHOR

DARYL S. PAULSON, Ph.D., is president and chief executive officer of BioScience Laboratories, Inc., a national testing laboratory facility located in Bozeman, Montana. He founded BioScience Laboratories in 1991 while developing and using the perspectives presented in *Competitive Business, Caring Business.* He is a member of the American Society for Microbiology, the American Psychological Association, and the Association of Practitioners of Infection Control. He is board-certified by the American College of Forensic Examiners, and has published more than thirty articles on clinical evaluation, business strategy, quantitative management science, the development of marketable products, experimental designs, microbiology, and psychology. Paulson received a bachelor's degree in business administration; a master of science degree in medical microbiology and biostatistics from the University of Montana, Missoula; a master of counseling psychology from the Human Relations Institute in Santa Barbara, California; a doctorate in psychology from Sierra University in Riverside, California; a doctorate in human science from Saybrook Graduate School and Research Center in San Francisco, California; and an M.B.A. from the University of Montana. Paulson was a Vietnamese-language interpreter in the Vietnam War, serving with the 1st Marine Division, headquartered near Da Nang. He was awarded the Combat Action Ribbon, the Navy Commendation Medal, with the Combat V for valor, and the Vietnamese Cross of Gallantry.

WANT TO KNOW MORE ABOUT PARAVIEW BOOKS?

A complete list of our books and ordering information are available at www.paraview.com. Paraview titles are immediately available on amazon.com, barnesandnoble.com, and other online bookstores, or you can order them through your local bookseller.

Leadership in a New Era
edited by John Renesch $16.95/£12.99
This collection of vision and wisdom for tomorrow's business leaders is presented by a group of outstanding men and women in a joint collaboration. This rare combination of business executives, professional consultants, successful authors, and leadership scholars has come together with a common theme: new times call for new leadership. Their collective voice calls for a fundamental transformation in the way we lead, the way we see leaders, the way we allow ourselves to be led, and how we think about leadership.

Paraview Press and **Paraview Special Editions** use digital print-on-demand technology (POD), a revolution in publishing that makes it possible to produce books without the massive printing, shipping and warehousing costs that traditional publishers incur. In this ecologically friendly printing method, books are stored as digital files and printed one copy at a time, as demand requires. Now high-quality paperback books can reach you, the reader, faster than ever before. We believe that POD publishing empowers authors and readers alike. Free from the financial limitations of traditional publishing, we specialize in topics for niche audiences such as mind/body/spirit, science, business, and balanced lifestyles. Please visit our website for more information: www.paraview.com.

Lightning Source UK Ltd.
Milton Keynes UK
11 June 2010

155405UK00002B/32/A